My Wild Woman:
A Sassy Spellbook for Women Who Want It All

Marian Singer

Adams Media
Avon, Massachusetts

Published by
Adams Media, an F+W Publications Company
57 Littlefield Street, Avon, MA 02322. U.S.A.
www.adamsmedia.com

ISBN: 1-59337-094-6

Printed in Canada.

J I H G F E D C B A

Library of Congress Cataloging-in-Publication Data
Singer, Marian.
Magick for the wild woman / Marian Singer.
p.   cm.
ISBN 1-59337-094-6
1. Magic. I. Title.
BF1611.S57   2004
133.4'3'082--dc22   2004001791

This publication is designed to provide accurate and authoritative information
with regard to the subject matter covered. It is sold with the understanding
that the publisher is not engaged in rendering legal, accounting, or other professional advice. If legal advice or other expert assistance is required, the
services of a competent professional person should be sought.
—From a *Declaration of Principles* jointly adopted by a Committee of the
American Bar Association and a Committee of Publishers and Associations

Many of the designations used by manufacturers and sellers to distin-
guish their products are claimed as trademarks. Where those designations appear in this book and Adams Media was aware of a trademark
claim, the designations have been printed with initial capital letters.

Illustration by Mona Daly

This book is available at quantity discounts for bulk purchases.
For information, call 1-800-872-5627.

To all the wonderful, wild women in my life who (by example) have taught me so much. In particular, my sisters who patiently handled teenaged angst even when I turned forty. Also, to all those women whose names I cannot begin to list and some I may never know, who have given service freely, boldly, and joyfully to myself or our community. Bless you for all you are and all you do.

Wild women: Those adventurous souls who go skydiving, effortlessly juggle home, work, and hobbies, and tackle life with confidence and verve. Have you ever wished you could be like that—even just a little?

Contents

Nine: Celebrate the Wild Woman 181

Appendix: Resources 193

Introduction

ild women: You know them—those adventurous souls who go skydiving and bungee jumping, those women who tenaciously tackle bulging budgets and land major accounts, or wear unique mix 'n' match clothing that makes its own fabulous fashion statement. Wild women also climb the corporate ladder, seem to effortlessly juggle children, home, and hobbies, and generally tackle life head-on with such power and confidence that you cannot help but admire them.

Have you ever secretly wished to live like that—just a little bit? Have you wished to let your hair down, get out of the doldrums, and really cut loose? Would you like to get your inner wild woman off the sidelines and out of wallflower status? Well then, it's long past time to start dancing to a whole new tune.

How? *Magick for the Wild Woman* is designed as a kind of textual music, aimed at getting those toes tapping and your spirit moving positively in a whole new direction. When you're feeling the need to banish uncomfortable situational trappings, such as bad habits, outmoded ideas, a poor self-image, and residual teen angst, *Magick for the Wild Woman* steps in with sound spiritual advice and activities that are tried and tested for success. Better still, this is a guilt-free book: no preservatives, no calories, and no one to prove anything to except, of course, yourself.

Despite what media hype might try to convey, there is no right or wrong type of woman except the type you want to be, starting today! No more feeling at the whims of fate. You are going to use practical magick proactively to start creating the life you've always dreamed about. It doesn't matter what your goal is—more money, feeling sexier and more confident, improving your business savvy, deterring bad luck, averting rivalry, or just generally having a little more fun in life—*Magick for the Wild Woman* offers reliable metaphysical methods for tapping that untamed, wild energy deep in your soul.

Why use magick for this job? Well, if you think back for a moment to the sorceresses, witches, and cunning people of old, you'll realize that such astute people have always lived on the edge, and seen the world from a different vantage point. They've dared to use their cleverness, cunning, intelligence, intuition, and sex appeal to grab hold of success no matter the setting. So why shouldn't you do likewise? Young or old, short or tall, big hair or no hair, every woman . . . every person, for that matter, should have the opportunity to stretch the boundaries of his or her life in any way that personal vision dictates. That includes you . . . yes, *you.*

Want to tap into your inner wild woman? First, stop putting your own needs into extended holding patterns. When you do this, it's like saying you're not important. In the long haul, such regular neglect leads to running out of gas, and emotional, physical, and spiritual crashes. Wild women have no intention of crashing and burning. Even when they do so accidentally, they always have a figurative first-aid kit ready, filled to overflowing with good humor, tenacity, and the awareness that tomorrow is, indeed, another day in the wild!

Secondly, watch your words. How often do you use phrases like "it's all on me" or "I'm only one person, what can I do?" Stop that cycle! Such words relinquish your power! Today is the day to reclaim your sacredness. You are a wild goddess in training.

Mind you, reconnecting with your inner goddess and wild energy may take a little time and effort. The road *Magick for the Wild Woman* maps out doesn't lead to some never-never land of perfection, and you won't always reach your goals quickly or easily. Instead, you'll internalize all the positive energy produced by your spiritual pursuits, and then carry it and express it wherever you may be. In the process, there are bound to be detours, potholes, and the usual assortment of daily frustrations to contend with. But with the strength and magick of your inner wild woman, you can do anything, achieve anything, and be anything. It's indeed a "wild" ride, but I can nearly promise, it will be fun and more than worth the effort.

Take a walk on the wild side today!

One

Myth Busters, At Your Service

Be brave enough to live creatively. The creative is the place where no one else has ever been. You have to leave the city of your comfort and go into the wilderness of your intuition. What you'll discover will be wonderful. What you'll discover will be yourself.

—Alan Alda

wild woman does not idly accept the myths and prejudices that history or society has left lying around to clutter up people's minds and perceptions. She secretly knows that it's all a bunch of hooey, and that real magick comes from creating a self-image that's really personal, meaningful, and empowering. It is also the wild woman's sacred task to undo those myths and quite literally sweep away their obnoxious clutter by living her life in a truly wild way.

However, to do this, we first need to examine the traditional image of womanhood and decide how it has affected us consciously, unconsciously, and socially. Then we can begin updating those images and redefining them so they make sense in our brave new world. Better still, we as women can also use our magick to root out the unproductive myths that have leeched onto our behavior and thought forms.

Myth #1: Women Are the Weaker Sex

Fact: Emotional, physical, and mental strength cannot be determined solely by gender.

Okay, ladies, anyone who has ever given birth can easily undermine this theory. I dare any man to squeeze a watermelon successfully out of his penis without crushing it! Yes, women's muscle structure is different and generally suited to different tasks, but that does not, in and of itself, indicate weakness. Weakness is a state of mind, and sometimes the way to overcome it is to elevate mind over matter. Think of the stories of women who without a second thought lift disabled cars to save their children. This is a potent illustration that reminds us of our inner, latent wild-woman powers—a strength that can turn around any weakness or problem in our lives. So dig deep and work with me now on busting those myths apart, and building something fresh, new, and fulfilling.

Activity: A Strength Charm

Metaphysically speaking, there are a variety of herbs, stones, and other objects associated with strength. For stones, you can consider amber, bloodstone, and loadstone. For plants and herbs, there are ash leaves, dill, fig, garlic, onion, pine, and thyme. Other potential symbols include a hammer, blood, the sun, as well as the colors yellow or red. From out of this list, you should be able to find a combination that's meaningful to you in making a special strength charm.

To give you an example, begin with a 4" × 4" yellow swatch of cloth. Inside the cloth, place a piece of bloodstone and loadstone to attract the energies you most want and need. Add some dried onion and garlic (about 1 teaspoon of each); the powerful aroma and taste of these items is associated with similarly strong vibrations. When you've gathered everything, put your hands palm down over all the items. Visualize a reddish-yellow light pouring from your palm into the entire assembly, and add an incantation like:

Stones so firm, stones keep me strong

Maintain this power where it belongs.

Garlic and onion hold me steady and sure

Keep the magick flowing and pure.

And when released into the winds

By my will, this spell begins.

Carry the pouch with you when you feel your inner resolve waning. When you need strength quickly, take a pinch of the garlic and onion and release it to the winds (you can also recite the incantation again to support your goal). When you get close to the bottom of the bundle, refill it and bless it anew.

Myth #2: Women Are Too Emotional

Fact: Strong emotions release endorphins, which have many positive benefits.

The warm, pleasurable feeling one experiences after sex is endorphin related. In fact, a lot of activities release these powerful hormones, including laughing, meditating, and eating really spicy food. Now if those sound like great pastimes, there's something even better you should know. These endorphins are actually good for your health. They enhance the immune system, relieve pain, reduce stress, and slow the aging process (to which every wild woman out there over the age of forty says a hearty huzzah!). So, the next time someone fusses over the fact that you laugh or cry, or feel things very deeply, just smile knowingly and make yourself look younger!

A wild woman's spiritual strength comes from her depth of emotions and sensations—those gut instincts that keep her from going awry, her ability to empathize without words, her compassion and nurturing. Yes, these are broad generalizations, but there is certainly nothing about these characteristics that any wild woman should disdain. The feminine or yin within our bodies can kick some serious butt on an emotional level. And when the endorphins are released, the physical follows suit. So try doing some "power feeling" instead of power lunches.

Let It Flow!

I know a lot of women who have shut down emotionally, in part due to this myth, and in part due to life's circumstances. When you find yourself going numb, when your emotional distance begins putting stress on relationships or your functionality, or when you can't seem to get in touch with your feelings, utilize a little wild willpower in combination with magick to help out.

For this activity, you don't need anything other than some undisturbed time when you can sit and meditate. For those of you who have trouble with meditation or visualization, I suggest tape-recording this activity ahead of time (or having a friend tape it). That frees your mind to really focus on the internal work instead of reading this page.

First, get comfortable. Close your eyes and breathe in deeply through your nose and out through your mouth. Release any tensions or worries. Turn all your attention toward that empty spot within. Don't be afraid to face it. Breathe through it as you might breathe through a cramp, knowing that the inner wild woman can fill that emotional void.

Next, imagine a pink-white light pouring down over your head. It's warm and seems to tickle all your senses. This is raw emotion. All those things you've pushed down, brushed away, or put up barriers against. Now it's time to let go!

Reach up for the light and welcome it. Embrace it as you would an old friend. Grab as much as your arms can hold and draw it into your heart chakra. Continue reaching for the light energy and moving it into your heart until you feel so full you could burst. If you feel like laughing, crying, or yelling, now's the time to do so! You've kept those feelings tucked away for too long. Reclaim them and the power that goes with them. Find comfort, strength, and self-awareness in what you feel and why you feel it.

After a while, this visualization makes most people weary (emotions use a lot of energy). So, when you want to "turn down" the intensity of what you feel and begin to return to normal awareness, put your strong hand (the one you write with) over your heart. Trace a counterclockwise circle over it, as if you were tightening the lid to a jar. You'll notice the amount of light shining out of the chakra slowly diminishes. Close it as much as you need to in order to cope with normal reality. Similarly, in the days ahead when you need to let some of those feelings out in a constructive, useful way, draw a clockwise circle to open up the flow!

Keep It Cool

A very wise friend told me that when you start feeling things, really feeling them, you feel everything for boon or bane. Now, the wild woman understands that not all emotions are good things, especially negatives like fear, hatred, or ire. Yes, we need to recognize our emotions, but they don't need to control us. The wild woman is always in the driver's seat of her mind and heart, ready to put on the brakes or use some clever magick when situations call for it.

In particular, I have very little tolerance for "button pressers"—you know, those people who purposefully try to tick you off? Until I became aware of it, such people always had the upper hand in my emotional life. They played me like a dancing puppet. So, I came up with a little spell to help me overcome my knee-jerk reactions, and take back the reins of control. Give it a try!

Find a red button (any size will do, but you want to be able to carry it with you easily). Wait until the Moon is waning, so that anger and your lack of self-control "shrink." Leave the button in the moonlight for three nights (the number three represents the balance of body, mind, and spirit). Each night when you place the button in the Moon's silvery beams, repeat an incantation like this three times. Fill in the blank with the name of the person or situation that constantly pushes your "button."

Anger's fire will never spark.

Like this Moon it grows cold and dark.

When _____ tests me like a fool,

keep my wits sharp and anger cool!

Carry the button with you whenever you go into that particular circumstance. If something occurs that you know is likely to stoke the fires, rub the button in your strong hand and think the incantation to yourself to release the energy.

Myth #3: A Woman Isn't Complete Without a Man (or a Partner)

Fact: Self-actualization is a stand-alone function.

We cannot complete anyone else's life until we complete our own.

As the saying goes, life is what we make it. It is long past time to seize the day in the temple of your own life. The only problem wild women face is that the negative influences on their behavior aren't always obvious. Additionally, discovering what those negatives are doesn't always help undo any collateral damage. For example, many women (and men, too) bemoan their single state because they're lonely and then turn around and unconsciously destroy a good relationship when it comes along. It's like the push-me/pull-you—we want what we perceive as a "have-not" and forget how much energy and ongoing effort serious relationships require.

My advice to anyone struggling with loneliness or just feeling out of the loop when all your friends are dating or married is to relax. Intimate relationships are not an immediate necessity for wild women so long as there are good friends around. In fact, very often the wild woman would rather give her prime-time energy to self-development and making herself happy. When a wild woman does this, everything else happens naturally! In fact, when you stop looking for partners and turn your attention to self-actualization, that's usually when someone comes rambling in and captures your heart.

Self-Actualization Anointing Oil

When animals mark their territory, they do it with natural oils or digestive by-products. The scent of both is wholly unique to a creature, akin to a fingerprint. Now, since you're taking charge of your life and focusing on *you*—the territory you want to mark is your body and your living space, basically reclaiming it as sacred and wholly yours.

These days it seems we spend very little time at home, and even less time thinking of it, or our bodies, as something special and sacred. Nonetheless, home is, indeed, where the heart is. This is the space within which the wild woman can be wholly herself and express that self without apology. It is also an altar upon which she can nurture her spirit to perfection. Likewise, our bodies are the temples of our souls. Thus, taking time to bless and mark these two things seems well worth the effort!

To begin you'll want to pre-prepare your anointing oil. What goes in it? Well, ask yourself about all the energies you want surrounding your body and your home. Things that immediately come to my mind are joy, love, peace, health, and a little fun! You can go to most bookstores and find guides that will list herbs and the qualities/energies associated with them. However, to start, you can try apple, rose, vanilla, and ginger to begin your magick!

Steep your chosen ingredients in 1 cup of warm (not hot) olive oil. The proportion of one teaspoon of each herb to the cup of oil is best. Steep and smell. If you're happy with the resulting scent, strain the oil and put it into an airtight container. If you'd like it stronger, strain the oil, add more herbs, and repeat the process. By the way, you may wish to add an incantation while stirring the oil clockwise to focus your energies. One example would be as follows:

From without to within, from head to toe

Keep safe this space; good fortune bestow

Fill every cell with love, joy, and peace

And may these blessings never cease!

Once made, this oil lasts about six months, provided you keep it cool and store it in a dark place.

Take your oil out and use it on yourself or your living space any time you feel a little "invaded"; for example, when you're visited by company who won't leave, when you need a boost of personal energy and confidence, or when you'd just like to spread around some good personal vibes. Honestly indulge yourself! Pour some of the oil into a long hot bath and revel in your aura. Feel really at home in your skin and your space, and celebrate all that is YOU!

Confidence Cooler

Some people rush into relationships out of fear that they will never find someone who really loves them again. This should send up an immediate warning flag in the wild woman's mind. For one thing, this behavior implies a lack of self-love and confidence, which are the first two things wild women strive to develop. Those attributes are the building blocks for healthy giving and receiving. So before you go jumping into the proverbial hot tub of love, check the water temperature and make yourself this cool-headed drink!

Place 1 cup raspberries (protective), 1 cup ginger ale (uplifting and energizing), 1 cup crushed ice (to keep your cool), a mint leaf (for clarity), and a few slices (about one-third) of banana for courage into a food processor or blender. Turn the setting to high and focus intently on your goal. Add an incantation like this one:

> Let my mind be clear, free from worry,
>
> free from fear. Love I'm worthy to receive,
>
> in this I trust and truly believe.
>
> If this path is good, let it be clearly understood.
>
> If this path leads to bane,
>
> let my interests immediately wane.
>
> So mote it be.

Drink this just before your next date with the person in question.

Myth #4: Beauty Is Only Skin Deep

Fact: Beauty is a state of the soul.

Many women spend a fair portion of their lives hating the reflection in their mirrors. The media saturate our senses with images of the prevalent conceptions of beauty, and somehow a normal, healthy wild woman often finds herself wanting. Why? Because we have a completely different measure of what's really important and that measure begins in our heart. There is no need to waste precious time thinking we are not "beautiful enough"—because quite honestly most of what humans perceive is only skin deep. Like a fanciful Barbie doll—it's plastic, made up, without value.

Philosophers in various eras have pondered the issue of beauty. Plato felt true beauty began with simplicity. Pythagoras said beauty in its ideal form was simply the foundation of form and structure that created an innate potential in all things. Pliny the Elder spoke of expression, posture, sentiments, and carriage as factors in what we consider beautiful. Immanuel Kant detailed beauty as a universal principle of nature that touches human hearts. And while all these outlooks have viable potential and offer a part of the bigger picture, the truest beauty to me is that which lies in the soul.

Okay, I know . . . saying that we're all beautiful in our own way is a heck of a lot different than truly trusting in those words and feeling them vibrate throughout our being. So how can we use a little metaphysical energy to help us with this goal? This activity is one that I've found helpful, and think you may, too!

Activity: Self-Blessing Mirror

I find it interesting that even in people's prayers, they'll ask for blessings for everyone *but* themselves. It seems that for all our spiritual evolution, we still overlook who is most important to the development of true beauty, true holiness—*ourselves!* If that sounds pompous, it's not. We are sacred beings, and we need to begin treating ourselves with that kind of respect. The purpose behind this activity is that of setting up a fresh, new pattern in our lives . . . one where we welcome blessings for ourselves so that beauty can shine from the inside out.

Try enacting this activity at least once a year, on your birthday or another date very special to you. More often is better, but what's most important is that you start making it (or an adaptation of it) part of your spiritual routine. For this activity, you need a full-length mirror and anointing oil or rose water. Begin by taking off one piece of clothing at a time as you face the mirror. With each item, release something about your self-image that isn't positive. When you're completely naked, pause for a moment and revel in the wonderful machine of your body. No matter the small imperfections—your body is your temple—this is your vehicle for learning in this lifetime. Honor it! Love it!

Next, pick up the oil or rose water and put some on the pointer finger of your strong hand. Dab this first on your feet, legs, hips, stomach, heart, third eye, and top of your head. As you stop at each spot (which are also power centers on your body), add a prayer-blessing to the Deity of your choice. One example that you can adapt to your own needs goes like this:

Goddess, bless my feet

to stay firm on the Path of Beauty

Goddess, bless my legs,

that they will not lead me astray

Goddess, bless my center of gravity,

to build strong foundations

Goddess, bless my heart

that I might give and receive love freely

Goddess, bless my vision to see promise

and potential, Goddess, bless my mind

that I might hear and see your messages

So be it.

By the way, you can keep the oil or water with you and dab a bit on any energy center when you feel the need to activate the blessings you've evoked.

Myth #5: Men Are More Logical and Better Suited to Leadership

Fact: There have been many cultures with strong, significant matriarchal influences that were honored and valued.

Just for the fun of it, I put the words *women leadership* into a search engine. It returned some 2,690,000 results! This really isn't surprising when we realize that women have taken on leadership roles for millennia. There are global accounts of women in authoritative positions of power. We also have accounts of civilizations in which women were free to act as individuals, without having to subordinate themselves. Here are a few examples:

North Africa: In the Tuareg tribe, women could pursue any romantic involvement they wished. When the husband was not home, other sexual company was welcome. If a divorce occurred, women retained custody of the children, and tents and furnishings were considered personal property.

West Africa: On the Bijagós islands near Guinea-Bissau, we find a matriarchal family structure. Women here can divorce and marry at will. The children receive the mother's last name, and the entire village and the education of the children are in the women's charge.

Arabia: Before Muhammad came on the scene, the Bedouin women could choose one or several husbands, whomever they desired. Yemen also had many female rulers, of which at least two remained well into Islamic times.

Egypt: We learn from Diodorus (a Sicilian historian) that Egyptians ordained that queens should have greater power and honor than a king, and that the wife should have authority over her husband. Some women, such as Hatshepsut, gained the power of the pharaoh and significantly improved agriculture and trade among her people.

Tibet: At one time Tibetan women took several husbands, while remaining the head of the household.

Japan: On Okinawa, women were traditionally the religious leaders and shamans responsible for all spiritual observances. Certain readings state that samurai envoys to the island were upset at having to present their credentials to the women of the court. Women still serve as religious leaders in this region today.

Although there are many more examples I could cite, you get the picture. Women have been highly successful leaders in a wide variety of social and cultural settings. They have also often found themselves in settings where there was no need to marry, to have a mate, or to relinquish control over personal goods to another. Such examples stand as a testament to the wild woman who is ready to take charge of her reality.

Activity: The Shout of Power

In the Far East, predominantly Japan, warriors used what was called a shout of power or *kiai* to tap into their inner resources. Knowing when to use this and how to execute it properly can become a great tool for the wild woman.

Begin by focusing on your belly button (the center of your gravity and seat of personal power). Fill your lungs slowly, thinking of the air as filled with the vibrations of the strength you need. Next exhale quickly. As you do, make a one-syllable sound (such as a vowel— *I I I, E E E,* etc.). The idea is to keep the shout short but incredibly loud. This is *not* yelling, and it shouldn't hurt your throat. If it does, you're doing it incorrectly. You'll know you've got it when the air is gone from your lungs afterward and you feel the adrenaline pumping in your system. When faced with a physical fight, the kiai keeps you from having the wind knocked out of you—so symbolically this is all about staying on your feet and facing things head-on!

An alternative to the kiai is the use of affirmations. Simple phrases like "I am strong" or "I am confident" recited outwardly have powerful vibrations. This energy saturates your aura and begins the process of positive change. If the situation doesn't permit you to vocalize your affirmations, simply think the phrases as often as possible. Thoughts are simply words uttered inwardly.

Myth #6: The War Between the Sexes Must Continue

Fact: Wild women choose their battles wisely.

The concept of a war between genders has left a lot of scars and bad feelings on all sides of the equation. There are enough important battles to commit our energies to, so why add another one that's really based on old gender-oriented myths and competitions? Wild women do not hate men, rather they see people as *people*—each with something special and unique to offer. In truth, while our physical housing has a male or female presentation, our personal attributes are a blend of both genders. It has been in failing to recognize that truth in times past that many problems between the sexes began.

So how do we begin writing a peace treaty between the sexes? We can start by releasing unrealistic images and expectations we have for ourselves and other women. Healing the rift between genders has to start within—in our perceptions, and in the way we act on those perceptions.

Sit down and ask yourself—what do you expect from yourself as a woman in the next week, the next year, the next five years? What image do you hope to create? Write down the answers, and set them aside for a minute.

Next, take a deep breath and pretend you're watching a movie. Pick up the list and reread it from a detached perspective. Which things on that list are unhealthy (if you're not sure, pretend it's your best friend's list—what advice would you give her)? Which items truly make you unhappy? How many goals place such excessive demands on your time and energy that you can't possibly handle them without getting sick or neglectful of other things? By paring down this list, you're slowly but surely signing that peace treaty in your own heart. How? By liberating yourself from unhealthy gender-oriented expectations and freeing yourself simply to *be*. At this juncture, you'll find it becomes much easier to do the same for the other men and women in your life.

Myth #7: Sexual Activity Equates to Wanton Ways

Fact: Sexuality and sexual expression are a sacred right for people of all genders and persuasions.

How many times is a sexually active man with several lovers called "virile" while a woman who similarly explores her passions is considered a harlot or tease? This is a concept that seems to have taken root around the 1600s. Women were thought to be amoral sexual predators whose animal drives had to be restrained by the more "advanced" and civilized creature known as man. Remember: the wild woman doesn't buy myths designed to paint women as sex objects or make them feel guilty about physical expression.

Myth #8: The Successful Woman Wears a Proverbial Red Cape

Fact: Wild women know their strengths and weaknesses and honor both in the way they live.

There has been an odd lingering misconception that any woman who succeeds in business or other "male" venues must be an overachiever. Obviously that's not true, but it does point to a potential flaw in the wild woman archetype. Sometimes in tapping our wild self, we try too hard, do too much, and overextend our reach. Our excitement and enthusiasm has to manifest somewhere, so one wild woman might become the workaholic, another the PTA partner and planner, and another still the towering stage mom. This is one myth that offers us a great opportunity to gauge ourselves and measure our pace. Make sure that the path you're on is uniquely yours as opposed to one imposed by expectations.

Additionally, this myth gives us pause for *pausing!* To work magic effectively, and keep your inner wild woman fully empowered, you must combat stress and weariness. If that means power napping, or taking time to meditate briefly on your lunch hour to refill your inner well, then do it! And don't forget a prayer before you go to sleep that focuses your energies on recharging. Perhaps something like this:

_____(insert divine name of your choice),

Let my slumber be true and deep;

Let my dreams be filled with light and beauty;

Let my body relax, my mind be still,

And my spirit be refreshed

So I will wake renewed.

You are your most important magickal tool; don't neglect self-care.

Summary

An exploration of gender-oriented myths is worthy of several books. My hope here is that this process uncovered other such myths for you—myths that have snuck into your mind or spirit. More important, I hope you've begun to root them out so the garden of your soul can really grow into that blossoming wild woman you seek.

Two

The Call of the Wild: Magick Round the Clock

In literature it is only the wild that attracts us. Dullness is but another name for tameness. It is the uncivilized free and wild thinking in *Hamlet* and the *Iliad,* in all the scriptures and mythologies, not learned in the schools, that delights us. As the wild duck is more swift and beautiful than the tame, so is the wild-mallard-thought, which 'mid falling dews wings its way above the fens. A truly good book is something as natural, and as unexpectedly and unaccountably fair and perfect, as a wildflower discovered on the prairies of the West or in the jungles of the East. Genius is a light which makes the darkness visible, like the lightning's flash, which perchance shatters the temple of knowledge itself, and not a taper lighted at the hearth-stone of the race, which pales before the light of common day.

—Henry David Thoreau

Once a wild woman has banished the demons of worn-out images and unrealistic expectations, she can start thinking about the here-and-now differently. One of the common sayings among magickally minded folk is that you should live the magick, not periodically dust it off like a useless knickknack. What does that mean to a wild woman? It means you are a goddess! From waking to sleeping, and every moment in between, your unique magick touches everyone and everything in and around your life.

Okay, now some of you may be wondering exactly how you go about making a mundane routine even remotely magickal. First, realize that humans are creatures of habit. We follow patterns every day of our lives. These patterns can be regarded as minirituals.

Just think for a moment. Your days typically follow a specific sequence of events. You walk through the house in the same way, take the same routes to work, park in the same area, and so on. These are, indeed, rituals, and when these rituals get disrupted everything feels a bit off. One of the goals of a wild woman is to adjust her perspective to include her soulful goals. Just because this "ritual" has mundane overtones, doesn't mean it isn't sacred. For one, it reveals a lot about your values and ethics. For example, if you are a slave to deadlines, you are also dependable and you respect other people's time (i.e., you are rarely late). More important, those patterns are already meaningful to you; in magick, meaningfulness is part of a potent trinity that also includes focus and willpower. These three energies working in tandem yield success!

With that reality in mind, here are some ways to go through your daily routines in a new, spiritually mindful manner.

Wake Up on the Wild Side

You know that old saying about getting up on the "right side" of the bed? This aphorism was born during the Roman era; they believed that gods presided over various sides of the body—the right side being more propitious! You can use this idea and combine it with other morning minirituals to encourage a little ongoing fortune throughout the day.

For example, I'm not the best morning person. Do not get between the coffeepot and me (and don't even think about using my "special" cup), or prepare to suffer the consequences! However, there's nothing that says I can't make the process of getting up and getting to what I jokingly call my altar for Caffeina a little more magickal. Here's one approach to try.

To begin, *do* get up on the right side of the bed. If possible, move clockwise through your home making your way to the coffeepot or teakettle. Clockwise or sunward movement generates positive energy. As you walk, recite affirmations to yourself—anything that's suited to the day ahead. For example, if you have a big meeting later in the day, try "I am confident" or "I have presence." Now comes the best part (for me, anyway)—enjoying that first sip of your favorite morning beverage. But before you internalize the liquid, stop and empower it by reciting an incantation into the cup:

A little luck, a touch of the wild

A little joy, a hint of style!

At work and play

Throughout my day

All good things shall come my way!

The wonderful thing about coffee and tea is that they both already have the symbolic value of being a "pick-me-up" and they motivate the energies of courage, stamina, and overall alertness. You're just putting those energies in motion with a touch of magick, then internalizing them as you drink!

Welcome the Wild Goddess

In our rush to get up and going, we often overlook taking even one brief moment to welcome the Divine into our day. The Wild Goddess isn't a pushy broad. She honors your sacred space and your boundaries. But if you are going to take your spirituality off that dusty shelf and actively use it in your life, then you need to find at least a couple of seconds to let Deity in!

My approach to this is to come downstairs, let out the dog, put on the coffeepot, and then go to my altar. I have one white candle I keep there as a symbol of Spirit. As I light it, I may say, "Morning, Mom!" offer a brief prayer, or express a need…whatever feels right at that moment. No King James verses necessary!

Note that this activity isn't fancy or time-consuming. What's important here is that little actions can change the way your entire day unfolds. Rather than having to do it all yourself, you've opened the door for the Goddess to remain as a copilot in your destiny. You've also opened the door for the Universe to work with you and through you during the day.

Don't worry. This doesn't mean that suddenly you'll have people seeking you out as a guru. Quite honestly, I've found the changes I see in my days are small, but very significant. The person at the supermarket who forgot her shopper's card (and I could lend mine), the child whose shoes I tied because Mom's arms were full, the call made on my cell phone for assistance for a traveler with a broken-down vehicle—such opportunities seem more plentiful when I wake up with the Goddess and welcome her into my heart and day. Give it a try! Practicing random acts of kindness and beauty are certainly high on the list of good guidelines for any wild woman's life.

Wish Well, Wish Often

Wishing is a very old and user-friendly form of magick. We wish on stars, on birthday candles; we wish on coins tossed in a fountain—and no one thinks much of it. However, wishing is a type of will-driven mechanism; its familiarity and simplicity make it very functional to the wild woman on the go. There are many ways to utilize wishing. As part of the daily routine though, there's one approach that works well for me, and you may like it, too!

Near my front door I keep a bowl with a candle anchored in the middle of it. The color of the candle represents my goal (and that candle remains in place until it's expended). Every morning before I head out on a task, I light the candle, express my wish, and put loose change into the bowl. When I can no longer light the candle, I give the change to a worthy cause. That cause may be a charity of choice, or a friend in need—it doesn't really matter as long as it's a selfless act. Always leave *one* coin in the bowl, and give the rest away. This is to bring the energy back, so the wish gets answered. Remember the Universal Law that everything you put out, be it negative or positive, returns to you threefold. Give it a try! When you make your bowl, you can add an incantation while affixing the candle to the bottom with wax. Recite something like this a number of times:

> Coins for gifts, coins that shine
>
> By my will, my wish fulfill,
>
> In each coin my spell I bind
>
> Wishes in the candlelight, wishes manifest,
>
> By the law of three, and blessed be's,
>
> I put my magick to the test!

Make sure that the bowl is fire-safe and don't place it where pets and children can easily knock it over. Place a trivet or hot pad below the bowl to avoid damage to surfaces from any transferred heat.

Great Squat, I Need a Spot

You've gotten the day started in a wonderful way, and now it's time to get to work. Those of you who drive, especially in crowded cities, know the frustration of not being able to find a decent parking spot. Typically some numb-nutz has parked crosswise in a spot that could easily hold two cars, or worse, someone pulls into a spot you've been waiting for. Facing this type of situation can really set your teeth to grinding, and ruin the positive energy you've generated. So, in a truly wild woman way, get proactive and avoid the problem with a little parking spell.

It's really quite simple. My "goddess" for good parking spots is named De-meter (hyphen purposeful). While this is an obvious pun, this spell always works so I'm not going to knock a good thing! Take a quarter in your hand. Promise De-meter the quarter for her assistance. When a parking spot opens up, and you leave your car, make sure to feed someone else's parking meter with that quarter. This is very important, even if it has to wait until later in the day—always, always give De-meter her due or the magick will not work for you again.

What's neat about this spell is that it is a random act of kindness that will make someone else's day a little more pleasant (which of course is good karma too!). Along the same lines, another spell that works fairly consistently is simply chanting, "Great Squat, I need a spot" while you're driving and looking (I believe that Squat is De-meter's male counterpart so you may wish to offer him a quarter as well!).

Mark Your Territory

I've worked in a lot of different situations, not all of them pleasant. Let's face it—you just can't choose your coworkers, and some of them can be downright annoy-ing. You know the types: the person who constantly taps his fingers, the perky jerk who has to be the expert on everything, the eternal butt-kisser, and so on. Now, wild women don't like to lose their cool (not to mention, it doesn't do a lot for your corporate image!). That's where you might find this activity quite helpful.

On days when you don't want to deal with anyone but those you *need* to deal with, bring this special oil to work. Now, you can use perfume instead of homemade oil if you want, but whatever you choose needs to have personal resonance for you. Next, go to work a little early (so you can do this when folks aren't watching). Dab the perfume or oil as you move counterclockwise around your office or cubicle. You are effectively marking your territory much as animals do. As you move, repeat an incantation such as:

This is my space

Negativity erase

Keep coworkers at bay

All negativity away!

Know that it's not necessary to speak an incantation aloud for it to work. Thoughts are words spoken inwardly and have just as much power as long as your will and focus remain sure. So if you feel as though your wall of privacy is losing some potency throughout the day, repeat the incantation in your mind to reinforce it.

Lunch and Leisure

Whenever you're breaking for a meal at work, you can also take a break to feed your spirit! For one, consider making yourself some magickally charged munchies so you can internalize the energy you most need. Chapter 4 has specific ideas and recipes along those lines.

Second, if your break is short, try some mental affirmations as you chew, or perhaps a prayer. Also breathing fully and evenly while you eat is an excellent way of de-stressing as well as helping avoid indigestion. Be mindful of breathing in positive energy, and releasing that which you don't need.

Last, if you have a little more time, bring a spiritually oriented book to read. Or, take fifteen minutes to meditate. Research shows that regular meditation not only helps regulate blood pressure, but it also improves overall energy and outlook, and decreases the instances of anxiety-oriented disease. Sounds like a recipe for success for any wild woman!

Sports Savvy

One of the first steps to being a successful wild woman is learning to truly enjoy life. The key is figuring out what really makes you happy and then providing yourself with ample opportunities to explore it. In particular, I've noticed more women turning to sports as an outlet for excess stress, and to stretch their limits physically. At the end of the day the wild woman might go for a hearty jog, play racquetball, shoot some hoops, or whatever. And while you may need to practice patiently to improve your skills in many of these sports, you can always carry a good luck amulet to provide a little boost of energy and confidence!

Try something that somehow ties into your sport and is easy to keep with you as you play. For example, you could tie magick into your sneaker laces! I've always loved the symbolism of knot magick because you can easily visualize the energy being held within the knot (or being released when you open it!). If you'd like to try this approach, knot the sneaker laces in between each eyelet as you recite a charm like this:

With the knot of one, my spell's begun

With the knot of two, my skills are true

With the knot of three, bring good luck to me

With the knot of four, my confidence restore

With the knot of five, this magick's alive!

Whenever you go to tie your sneakers, you can mentally recite the charm to release its energy into your sporting efforts!

Undress to De-stress

How many of us indirectly bring home the bad vibes of disgruntled coworkers, rude people on the highway, and other similar aggravations. We walk right into our houses bearing all that negativity! Who needs it? Certainly not the wild woman!

There are things you can do to wash away the day's energy residue. As soon as you get in the door, take off your shoes (kind of like kicking the negative dust off your feet). Next, go to a dressing area and take off the rest of the work-a-day gear. With each item you remove, also release a point of stress in the day. Name each item after that nagging, lingering energy that you want to release from your aura. Drop the item into a hamper with a sachet of a cleansing aromatic—lemon rind or pine needles are two good choices. Chapter 3 has more ideas on aromatic magick.

If you want, you can chant something like this as you're undressing:

Away, away, all negativity at bay
Only good energies are here to stay.

Or simply take a deep breath and repeat *OM* (which means "I am"—the perfect way to reclaim the sacred space of self after a long day).

Now don't look at the clothes and don't accept that negativity back. Rather, stretch and breathe. Take at least five minutes to purposefully relax your muscles and mindfully enjoy the fact that you're back home, in your sacred space. Finally, get on fresh, fun clothing. I'm willing to bet you feel better for it!

Mealtime Magick

The day is done and it's time to sit down for dinner. For those of you who don't really "sit" during dinner, I highly advocate adding at least two real, at-the-table-type dinners a week. We spend way too much time rushing hither and yon. Stopping for a decent meal with family and friends in the midst of chaos can become a great coping mechanism, not to mention an opportunity for making magick.

We'll talk a little more specifically about planning and preparing thematic menus in Chapter 4. At this juncture, I just want to talk about dinner. You can tackle your mealtime magick in one of three ways: prepare some blessed food over the weekend and freeze it, make something fresh based on wild whimsy, or use a packaged meal to which you bring a little crafty witchery!

The key here is thoughtfulness and meaning. What does your food communicate to you in terms of symbolism? For example, when I want to feel "in the pink,"

I'll have pink grapefruit juice as a beverage. When I want to feel really content, I make Mom-styled roast beef (my mom always seemed really happy when she cooked it). So, start with your memories and experiences when considering exactly what to prepare for mealtime magick. What are your comfort foods? What things do you really like to cook? Your pleasure and comfort will likewise translate into the food, and you'll internalize all that good energy as you eat what you've prepared.

Now, sometimes it's impossible to make a full meal. I've been known to resort to hot dogs and macaroni and cheese on many a night. But there's magick in those, too. Cheese is a love food—and what wild witch doesn't need a little more love? Hot dogs can be cut and placed on the plate like a smiley face to please the child in each of us. Stir clockwise as you prepare the food to bring blessings. Recite a little ditty if you wish:

Noodles and cheese, life's a breeze
With butter and sauce, magick is tossed!

Pray over the edibles before serving them, charge each item with good energy, play some nifty New Age music, and eat expectantly! Again, the wise wild woman knows that things need not be fancy to be functional and fulfilling!

Bed Blessings

How often do you wake up in the middle of the night and have no idea why? For many spiritual people, the reason boils down to not taking the proper time to shield themselves psychically before they go to sleep. Consider how many people drive by your home angry, upset, or otherwise out of sorts. How often are your neighbors fighting or under stress? What about stressful situations from your day that may be lingering in your aura? All those energies can easily intrude on your rest. Why? Because most people are more open to empathic and psychic impressions while they're sleeping. When you sleep, your body slows down, your mind can sort through all the impressions of the day, and Spirit can get a word in edgewise!

There are many ways to help ensure a good night's rest so you can wake up wild and refreshed the next day. First, have a cup of relaxing tea. Catnip, chamomile, and mint are three options. While you're sipping, stir the tea counterclockwise imagining that your stress is going away like so much liquid down a drain and out of you.

Before changing into your pajamas, toss them into the dryer for a minute or two with some relaxing herbs tied into the toe of some old pantyhose. Lavender makes a nice touch. If there's little time for this, or you don't have a dryer, consider having some type of restful aromatic present in your room in the form of incense, potpourri, or a sachet. Some of the herbs recommended to improve sleep include chamomile, hops, lavender, peppermint, thyme, and violet. If you're bundling any of these into a sachet, wrap them in a bit of cotton with a dab or two of aromatic oil for longevity. The cotton also keeps random pieces of herbs from poking through the cloth.

Now just as you stretched out when you came home today, try stretching again before bed, remembering to breathe deeply and evenly. Shake out all that tension (if you're wearing your shoulders like earrings, you are *not* relaxed!). Turn off the lights and phone, and get comfortable in bed.

As you lie there, visualize yourself surrounded by a lovely white-blue light that shimmers gently. This is a soft, glowing image (as opposed to bright daylight) akin to dusk in illumination level. The light is warm and comforting, like your favorite blanket. Hold that image in your mind as you fall asleep. It creates a shield in your aura against those wandering bits of energy I spoke about. If that imagery doesn't work for you, try seeing yourself in a protective bubble. Or, perhaps mentally paint your walls, ceiling, and floor with glowing protective emblems.

Now some people have trouble with visualization. If you're among them, don't be discouraged. There are other ways to safeguard your sleeping space metaphysically without using that particular method. For one, you can create an informal sacred space in your room by inviting the energies of Earth (North), Air (East), Fire (South), and Water (West) to watch over your magick. If you choose this approach, select four small items that you charge specifically for that purpose. I have a 1"-tall pewter dragon for fire, a silver coin for earth, a seashell for water, and a feather for air. In choosing items, find things that reflect the element/direction they represent. Another option for fire, for example, might be a candle or matches. To charge the items, expose each to the element to which it corresponds. If the fire item would be damaged by heat, you can move it through smoke instead. As you introduce the token to its element, say, "I charge you with the protective power of _____ (insert the element)." When that step is done, take the four tokens to your room. As you put them in their respective locations, add an incantation such as:

Powers of North, South, East, and West

Upon my call, answer my behest

And with these tokens wrap around

Protect this room, let magick abound!

Repeat this incantation again three times (once each for your body, mind, and spirit) before going to bed.

Sweet Dreams

Once you've started down the path of walking on the wild side, a lot of things begin to change. At least one area in which you will probably notice a difference is your dreams, especially since you're being more conscientious about blocking out psychic clutter. They'll seem brighter, more dimensional, and more meaningful. This is perfectly normal, and something to celebrate.

If you'd like to encourage more spiritually oriented dreams, and those that come from your Higher Self and Spirit, there are ways of doing so. Better still, for the ever-busy wild woman this makes your sleep time more productive (I'm all for multitasking!). For one thing you can get yourself a dream catcher. In Native American traditions, these little webs strain out only bad dreams, leaving the best night visions for you to experience. If you can't find a dream catcher, you can make one out of lace doilies, feathers, crystal, and ribbon that are quite pretty and perfectly functional. As you knot in the decorative items, willfully capture any negativity there too. You can add a little rhymed incantation to the process like this one:

With knot one, my spell's begun

With knot two, the magick is true

With the knot of three,

only good dreams to me.

You can also consider the various aromatics used throughout history to aid inspired dreams. These include rose, jasmine, marigold, and balsam. By the way, if you'd like a multipurpose sachet, add some of these to the protective bundle you made in the last activity!

Finally, make sure you keep a tape recorder or paper and pen near the bed. Write down your dreams immediately on waking, as the details tend to disappear with time. Read this over later in the day and have a good dream interpretation book handy. You'll be surprised at how many dreams have messages for you, and how often Spirit has been trying to get your attention.

Summary

From sunup to sundown . . . from daybreak to dessert . . . from reading the morning paper to rituals . . . from seeing sunrise to finally sleeping again, you are a wonderful, wild, magickal Being. Celebrate her. Honor her. Respect her. Make your life the act of worship, and all else is icing on the cake.

Three

Spice Yourself Up

The more wild and incredible your desire, the more willing and prompt God is in fulfilling it, if you will have it so.

—Coventry Patmore

*S*omehow I cannot think of a truly actualized wild woman without thinking of words like *zesty, robust,* and *spicy.* However, the question remains, what exactly is the leavening that will encourage these actualized traits to rise fully into the surface of our being? There are several helpmates, many of which we'll explore in other chapters. For the moment, we'll turn our attention to various aromatics that will help you feel more alluring, exciting, confident, professional, or whatever impression you wish to convey.

Essentially, we're mingling magick with the art of aromatherapy. As an art, aromatherapy has been around since around 1500 B.C., when we find chronicles discussing the use of scents like lavender for medical purposes. Egyptians used aromatics to cure depression, Greeks considered them to be divine in origin, and many religious groups used aromatics in scenting sacred spaces.

During the Middle Ages, the great healer Hippocrates advocated aromatic baths as healthful. And although it wasn't until about sixty years ago that the term *aromatherapy* was specifically coined and brought into common usage, this brief overview gives you a feel for the rich heritage on which you can draw!

In particular, wise wild women of old understood the power of herbs and used this knowledge for everything from helping star-crossed lovers to healing cattle! In keeping with this diversified and highly creative tradition, you'll find simple and fun aromatic recipes here for things like the "I don't want to be Mommy today" incense and "rub me the right way" cream. The greatest beauty of it all is that magickal aromatherapy is subtle. Wild women can use it nearly any time, anywhere!

Magick in the Pantry

Before trying specific recipes, the wild woman must first prepare herself and her workspace for the task at hand. While you need not have a kitchen worthy of Julia Child, nor a pristine workspace that would please Miss Manners, ambiance and orderliness can have quite an impact on your magick. In particular, you're not going to want to stop in the middle of a spell-recipe to grab a forgotten ingredient, because that would deter your focus. So, get everything out in advance, take a few minutes to clean up the kitchen, and organize your work area logically. This time and effort is really no different than preparing for a ritual, only the kitchen is now your sacred space!

Speaking of sacredness, it's important that you find ways of stirring in a healthy dose of spirituality to your wild woman recipes. There are many examples of how to do that—but ask yourself which ones will work best for you. Does lighting a candle turn your mind toward magick? Playing New Age music or burning incense? When you discern what works, use that process regularly. Other ideas that you may find helpful in inspiring that spiritual focus include:

- Invoke the quarters (Invite the elemental powers of Earth, Air, Fire, and Water into your space) or welcome your Deity into the kitchen with you.
- Stir your preparations clockwise (the direction of blessings) while thinking about your needs and goals.
- Use special timing for the preparation process (like the full moon for completion and manifestation).
- Sing sacred music, chant, or recite affirmations.
- Wearing clothing that you might wear in ritual, or whose colors reflect the goal of your magick.

The key here, and it's pretty much the wild woman's mantra, is "meaningfulness equals successful magick." Your intention, focus, and ability to set aside the temporal and turn toward the eternal are what determine how successfully your recipe-spells turn out. Carry the vision of your sacredness into the kitchen with you, consider that space as a temporary temple, and you should do just fine.

Oils

Making your own anointing and cooking oils can be a lot of fun. For one reason, they become wonderful gift items because you can personalize the blend to whomever you wish. For another reason, you can make as much or as little as you need; the oils typically have at least six months of shelf life.

The basic recipe for oil is 1 cup of good-quality oil (virgin olive oil, almond oil, etc.) to ⅓ cup of dry herbs. Simmer this mixture, covered, over a low flame for at least two to three hours. Strain and check the strength of the aroma. If need be, you can add more herbs at this time and simmer again until you get the desired scent. Store this oil in a dark, airtight bottle in a cool spot. Make sure you label the oil: the ingredients and its intended function (this is doubly important if you make both culinary and ritual oils; the latter may have inedible ingredients).

By the way, you can use fresh aromatics, like flower petals or bark, for this process as well. Just be aware that some plants are very heat sensitive. So, put the plant parts into a clear bottle and cover them with oil; then place the container in a sunny window. Shake the bottle daily, adding an incantation that supports your goal, until the parts turn translucent; strain and store as before. This process takes more time, but you don't have to worry about overheating, and it gives you more opportunities to mingle in your magick! If your oil ever appears cloudy, do not use it. That means the oil has turned, which also "turns" the magick.

Toil Oil

This oil is designed to give you determination and strength when you have a lot of hard work ahead of you. Wild women know that hard work is good magick, but that doesn't mean you can't get some spiritual assistance! To keep up with your hectic schedule, this recipe uses refined aromatic oils, which are blended together.

½ cup saffron oil (an herb thought to improve physical strength)
2 drops cedar oil (courage)
2 drops rosemary oil (mental focus)
3 drops vanilla (power and health)
1 drop ginger oil (success)

1. Seal all the ingredients into the container in which you plan to store them. Hold this in your strong hand and repeat an incantation like this three times (once each for your body, mind, and spirit):

> Strong in spirit, strong in body, strong in mind
> Within this oil, my magick I bind
> When to the seat of courage applied
> There the magick and strength reside!

2. Apply this oil near your belly button. This is the center of your body's gravity and the region in which vigor resides.

Sexy and Sensual

As with the last blend, I've used essential oils that you can whip up quickly before a romantic encounter to use for mutual massages. If time allows, get fresh herbs and prepare it according to the basic recipe so it will be edible!

1 cup almond oil (for love)
3 drops vanilla oil or extract (lust and passion)
2 drops ginger oil (yang energy and overall lasting power)
2 drops violet water (yin energy)

1. If time allows, wait until the Moon is waxing to full to prepare this, as that improves the overall romantic energies. Once the oils are sealed in their container, shake them together saying:

> Powers of the West, hear this behest
> Release our passions; release our hearts
> Through this oil, desire impart.

2. Mentally recite this invocation again as you're massaging your partner, and let nature take her course!

Creams

As in making oils, you can hasten the process of making aromatic creams by simply taking any commercial brand and adding an essential oil to it. However, when time allows, it's worth making your own. The focus and personal energy you bring to the process improves the magick created!

The base for a cream can be coconut oil, cocoa butter, wax, petroleum jelly, aloe, oil, or a blend of any of these (the oil needs the wax or butter to give it more body). To 2 parts base, add 1 part dry herbs, or 1.5 parts fresh herbs (dried herbs are more concentrated). Essential oils can be added to personal taste as long as you have no skin sensitivity (cinnamon oil, for example, can be very harsh).

Warm the base over a low flame, adding your chosen components. Simmer for about ninety minutes and then strain it. Test the strength of the aroma and repeat with more herb(s) if necessary. When you've got the desired scent, you'll need to beat the base continually so it cools with a creamy texture. If it seems too solid, warm it slightly and add a little olive oil or more aloe and beat again.

Rub Me the Right Way

The components in this cream inspire hospitality, goodwill, and overall friendly exchanges between people, especially when things previously have been tense.

½ cup almond oil
¼ cup pineapple rind
1 orange tea bag
2 teaspoons dried lemon rind or powder
1 cup beeswax (pink is a good choice of colors to inspire friendly feelings)
2 tablespoons aloe gel

1. Warm the almond oil with the pineapple, orange tea, and lemon therein. Simmer until it takes on a strong aroma (add more herbs if needed). Strain and return to the stove. Add the beeswax and aloe, stirring constantly. Once the wax melts and blends with the other ingredients, remove the mixture from the heat and continue beating until cool. Remember to stir clockwise to inspire positive energy, and perhaps add a little chant like this one:

> Friendship and goodwill
> My magick fulfill
> Good energy spread
> Wherever I tread!

2. Transfer the cream to a jar with an airtight lid, and use as desired. You can warm this cream and use it for massages, too.

Smooth Sailing

We're using a little sympathetic magick here by applying a smooth cream first thing in the morning so that our day might likewise go forward smoothly!

½ cup cocoa butter
¼ cup coconut oil
2 tablespoons aloe (optional, but aloe has a strong healing quality)
⅛ cup lavender flower
¼"-slice fresh ginger root, mashed

1. Warm all the ingredients together, saying:

> Cream, cook quick, my magick behooves
> That each day is happy, healthy, and smooth!

2. Transfer the cream into a storage jar, label it, and apply as desired. By the way, you can dab both your creams and oils on light bulbs to literally turn on the magick you've created when you flip the switch (the heat will also release the aromatherapy into your living space).

Incense

Incense has an ancient history. It is mentioned on Egyptian tablets dating from 1530 B.C.E. and is also described in the Vedic literatures of India, which date from 5000 B.C.E. During those times, the most common components were natural aromatic woods such as sandalwood, and the essential oils of flowers and herbs. From this cradle of civilization, incense found its way into global religious practices. It is part of Buddhist meditations, Shinto temples, Christian rites, and Native American cleansings. Voodoo traditions use incense to aid visions and inspire prophetic dreams. This means the modern wild woman has a rich tradition on which to base her use of aromatics.

Remember, however, "more" does not equate to "better." Use no more than three additives in your blend and then test it to see how it burns. When you start putting a lot of different aromatics together, the results can be nasty (and how it smells dry can be dramatically different from how it smells while burning).

If you'd prefer to create cone incense, begin with 4 teaspoons of any aromatic wood powder. To this, add 1 teaspoon of gum arabic and 20 teaspoons of whatever dried herbs and plant matter you desire. Blend well. Next, add ¼ cup of saltpeter to this base. (You can find many of these ingredients at your local hobby or arts and crafts store.) Add ¼ cup of water a little at a time until it reaches a dough-like consistency. Shape this into whatever size cones you wish or shape them into something that represents your magickal needs or goals. Just make sure you leave a point from which to start the burning process. Dry the cones for at least three days before storing them away. As with the other products in this chapter, make sure you note the ingredients and the purpose for which the incense is made.

Day-Off Delight

This cone incense is designed to improve the overall vibrations for that well-deserved day of rest and relaxation. Light it, kick off your shoes, grab a cool drink, read a wild woman's book, and celebrate yourself!

4 teaspoons powdered catnip (for beauty and self-love)
10 teaspoons powdered lavender flower (for happiness, harmony, and peace)
1 teaspoon nutmeg (health)
3 teaspoons heather (for serendipity)
2 teaspoons ginger (to recharge your inner well)

1. Follow the instructions for the basic cones, adding the other necessary ingredients (namely, the wood powder, water, saltpeter, and gum arabic). If possible, create this batch in sunlight to inspire all the blessings you deserve, and then energize the blend with a chant such as:

> By the warmth of the sun, and its blessed light
> The power of my will and magickal might
> Fill this blend with pure delight!

2. Store the cones after they've dried completely and make sure to pack a few for your next vacation!

Peace Pipe Powder

Every home experiences tensions between the cohabitants periodically. When you find the stress in your living space begins to rob you of your wild whimsy, burn a little of this incense near the stove or fireplace to restore harmony in the home.

5 teaspoons dried gardenia petals, finely ground
5 teaspoons lavender flowers
5 teaspoons dried violet petals
5 teaspoons pennyroyal

Add these four ingredients to 2 cups of aromatic wood powder. I used 5 teaspoons of each ingredient to represent the power of the pentagram in balancing diverse energies. As you stir this mixture to mingle the herbs, charge it with energy by saying something like the following. (You can recite this when you burn it, too.)

> Smoke of healing, smoke of peace
> By my will, hostility—cease!
> Cleanse negativity through the winds
> When released with this chant, my spell begins!

Candle Craft

Candles are one of the most inexpensive and highly adaptable tools in the wild woman's kit. Not only does their light make everything look so much gentler, but they also have a variety of magickal applications. The ways in which you can blend metaphysics with candle burning include:

- Adding symbolic oils or herbs to the candle wax so the aroma and energies are released upon burning (like vanilla for joy and rose for love).
- Securing the candle on top of a small crystal chosen for its vibrational significance or placing the candle in a ring of crystals to amplify the energy (such as amethyst for peace or moonstone for psychic aptitude).
- Placing the candle in an elementally significant quarter of a space to illustrate your need or goal (alternatively, you can use the feng shui correspondences when considering placement).
- Choosing the candle's colors according to the theme of your magick (such as red for passion and yellow for communication).
- Carving meaningful symbols into the wax while focusing on your goal.
- Using wax drippings, or the flame of the candle itself as a divinatory focus by watching them for signs (for example, a bright flare-up of the candle's flame is considered a positive omen).
- Observing the flame of the candle as a meditative aid.

Unless you want to get really fancy, making your own candles is a relatively simple process. I still like using the milk-box method from my youth. You can get wax in most supermarkets with the canning items or at hobby stores. To begin, use an old pan to melt the wax and blend in whatever additives you've chosen. Candles with too many additives (or those that are not finely powdered) may not burn evenly or safely, so err on the side of being conservative, knowing you can always dab some oils on the wax before you light it. Also, keep the pan you've used set apart from your cooking gear and do not wash it in the kitchen sink (having to call in a plumber for wax buildup isn't fun).

Next, put just a little cooking oil on the inside of the carton (this helps with removing the candle later). Then, take a knife or a pencil that's long enough to go across the square opening of the milk carton and tie the wick to the middle. On the other end of the wick, tie something small and heavy so it stays centered when you pour the wax into the mold. Let the wax cool just a bit before transferring it to the carton. Once the wax hardens completely, if the oil doesn't release the candle without struggle, you can remove it easily by dipping the carton into a bucket of hot water!

Clarity Candle

I prefer to use plain beeswax for this candle; if that's not available, a plain white candle is a second option. Symbolically speaking, beeswax burns cleanly and clearly, just as you want your mind to function! Besides the wax, look to aromatics that enhance conscious awareness and logic such as the following:

- Grape
- Lily
- Mint
- Rosemary

For stones, your options include:

- Aventurine
- Calcite
- Fluorite
- Sphene

If you want to use a symbol, try a simple eye to represent vision!

Clarity is a solar function, so try to create this candle during daylight hours; noontime is best so that you shine the sun's full light on whatever situation is at hand.

Where mind and spirit need to peer

Let my vision be crystal clear

When thoughts and perspectives aren't quite right

Grant clarity, in this candle's light!

Use this candle in the sunlight and repeat the incantation as you light it.

Meditation and Muse

In contrast to the clarity candle, this one focuses on your inner well of creativity. It will help you move into deeper meditative states and tap some of that muse that often lies dormant.

Look to aromatics that facilitate inventiveness, serenity, and communication with your higher self such as:

- Allspice
- Jasmine
- Lavender
- Lotus
- Marigold
- Rose
- Sandalwood
- Grape
- Lily
- Rosemary
- Violet

For crystals, you might try:

- Amethyst
- Carnelian
- Geodes
- Lapis
- Sodalite

- Kunzite
- Blue tourmaline
- Aventurine
- Coral
- Moonstone

If you want to carve something in the wax, an image of the Moon is apt since it's tied to our spiritual natures. You want to work with a waxing or full moon for best results. I prefer blues and purples (if you want to add some coloring) for meditative candles. For this one, I added a hint of yellow to stress the creative aspect. An energizing incantation might go like this:

By my will and candle bright

Grant to me clear inner sight

From out the warmth of candle's light

Spark my muse with magick might!

You can repeat this to yourself as you light the candle and begin your breathing for meditation practices.

Potpourri

Potpourri and pomanders offer a wonderful alternative for fragrant magick if your skin is sensitive to oils or lotions, or your nose and eyes get itchy around smoke. Both potpourri and pomanders have a much subtler scent, and by utilizing essential oils from time to time, both have a very long shelf life. Of the two, potpourri is a simpler process. It consists of:

Aromatic leaves
Bark in large pieces
Dried berries
Essential oil to improve the scent
Flower petals
Fruit peelings
Orrisroot powder as a fixative

The proportions here are 1 tablespoon orrisroot to 1 quart mixed plant matter and however many drops of oil are necessary to create the strength of fragrance you find most pleasing. Placing the potpourri in sunlight improves the aromatic effect but will eventually bleach out the components and require more frequent refreshing with oils.

Pomanders

Pomanders come to us from medieval times when they were carried to ward off disease and the smell of people who did not bathe frequently. There are a variety of ways to make these, but one of the easiest is as follows:

1 part benzoin
1 part blended herbs
A little water to make a paste
A few drops of essential oil to improve the scent
A few drops of beeswax so the texture is even all the way through

Wrap the mixture in cheesecloth and infuse it with whatever energies are most needed. You can accomplish this by taking a deep breath from the center of your diaphragm and letting the air out slowly while focusing on your goal.

Harmony Hand Basket

You may want to put this gathering of aromatics in a cornucopia, which symbolizes abundance, or other decorative basket so you can pick it up and take it wherever it's most needed. Good choices for harmony include the following:

Cloves or cinnamon sticks (love)
Lavender or lily (joy)
Lime rind or pine needles (healing)
Violet or gardenia (peace)

Harmony is a very delicate process in which all the ingredients should be balanced to reflect your home and its uniqueness. For example, if someone in your space has experienced depression and that's throwing the harmony out of sync, you'll want more happiness-oriented components to inspire symmetry. Good choices would include any items with the color blue: hawthorn flowers, lavender, lily, and marjoram. If there's a way to add a candle to your harmony handbasket, even better, as light symbolically banishes darkness. Light the candle whenever the level of disruption in your home gets out of control. For a blessing, try something like this:

> Spirit of joy, spirit of peace
> May your blessings never cease
> Spirit of kinship, spirit of light
> Keep us ever in your sight.

Playful Pomander

The wild woman always has time for a little playfulness. Sadly, today's society doesn't always encourage that healing, healthful type of release. This little pomander helps keep a nice, steady stream of whimsical energy around your sacred space. You'll need the following:

1 teaspoon finely chopped feathers	Lily oil
¼ cup hawthorn flowers	¼ cup pink wax
Benzoin	Gauze
Water	Pink ribbon
Lavender oil	

1. Ask yourself what time of day your mind naturally turns to more playful matters. For me, I can finally relax after dinner. Whatever time that is for you, that's the best time to create this pomander. Take the feathers, flowers, benzoin, and water, and make a paste. Add the oils (according to personal taste, a few drops at a time) and pink wax, molding the blend together into a nice size ball. Your incantation might be something like this:

> Be the need come night or day
> Spirit, teach me how to play!
> And in this bundle, whimsy's bound
> When released to the winds, magick surrounds!

2. Wrap the bundle in the gauze until it fully hardens and secure it with ribbon, adding a loop at the top so you can hang this where it's most needed.

Wild Woman's Wish List for Aromatics

Here I've provided a list of aromatics, and their metaphysical applications, in alphabetical order. Use this handy reference list when you're looking for just the right smells to spice up your life (or a handy way to use an abundance of pantry spices).

- *Almond:* health, awareness, divinatory ability
- *Allspice:* serendipity, creativity
- *Anise:* zeal, overcoming nightmares, safety
- *Apple:* happiness, beauty, abundance, well-being
- *Basil:* dedication, love, joy
- *Bay:* success, strength, divinatory ability
- *Berry:* prosperity, luck, joy
- *Cedar:* purification, bravery, protection
- *Chamomile:* smooth transitions, stress buster
- *Cinnamon:* power, lust, clarity
- *Frankincense:* de-stressing, cleaning out negativity
- *Ginger:* energy, centering, communication
- *Grapefruit:* revitalization, easing depression
- *Heather:* taking hold of "fate," attractiveness, communication with spirits
- *Honeysuckle:* abundance, intuition, protection
- *Jasmine:* meditation
- *Lavender:* calm, restful energies, peaceful intentions
- *Lemon:* purity, refreshment, dedication, emotional balance

- *Lilac:* peace, conscious mind
- *Lotus:* focus on your spiritual (inner) life
- *Mint:* financial improvements, health, antianxiety, hopefulness
- *Myrrh:* recuperation, banishing
- *Orange:* restful sleep, health, fidelity, happiness
- *Peach:* sagacity, lasting results, wishes, truthfulness
- *Pine:* purification, banishing, health, victory
- *Pineapple:* hospitality
- *Rose:* love (all types), oaths, meditative focus, karmic awareness
- *Rosemary:* the conscious mind
- *Sage:* wisdom and purification, dream interpretation
- *Sandalwood:* confidence, the intuitive nature
- *Thyme:* psychic powers, bravery, health
- *Vanilla:* happiness, kinship, passion
- *Vetiver:* change, shape-shifting
- *Violet:* service, faithfulness, trust, calm

Summary

Bear in mind that this list is only a starting point. If an aroma has a different meaning for you, that is the meaning you, as a wild woman, should use in your magick. A wild woman always trusts herself, and her life's experiences, as her ultimate "guru" or guide in spiritual pursuits.

Four

Zen and the Art of Home Cooking

I believe you can have whatever you really want in this life, in one form or another, sooner or later. All you have to do is take care of your health and be lucky enough to live for a while. But you can't have it all at once and you can't have it forever. No life has the room for everything in it, not on the same day.

—Barbara Sher

*M*s. Sher's quote illustrates an important lesson for the wild woman: No matter how much living we might wish to cram into one lifetime, there are only so many hours in the day. None of us wants to burn out or fade away. That's why it becomes so important to find effective ways of mixing our spirituality into everyday, routine things. The kitchen is the perfect place to start.

While you might not immediately equate the kitchen with the wild woman's philosophy, it can certainly be a big part of it. The basic process isn't difficult at all. Most of it comes from approaching your cooking space with a different demeanor—one that's spiritual rather than mundane. Think back to the times when your grandmother (and her mother before her) did everything in the kitchen, from making daily meals, to tending to broken bones, to telling stories and teaching family tradition. Both multitasking and recognizing sacredness wherever it can be found are definitely in the wild woman's credo.

Since you have to eat anyway, why not blend a little magick into the equation? In this case, consuming what you've prepared helps you internalize the energy! Spiritually enhanced food feeds a wild woman's soul as well as her body and gives her the energy necessary to express herself fully and completely.

To show you how to create those special energies in your kitchen, I'm providing a couple of different recipes in a variety of traditional categories that could be found in nearly any recipe book. The big difference here is that the components chosen for these items have symbolic meaning to the overall dish, while the method of preparing them gives you a way to focus your intention and saturate your edibles with magick!

Energizing Additives

The word *additive* in, and of, itself has great potential from a symbolic point of view. Rather than just adding flavor, you're adding energy to the mix! Savory salts are easily prepared by simply mixing finely powdered herbs into the blend. For example, I have one blend that includes orange powder, garlic, lemon powder, onion powder, and kosher salt. It's fabulous on chicken and fish, and bears a very protective, healthy energy signature.

The basic process for making aromatic oils (as covered in the last chapter) works for culinary ones, too! Try a mixture of bay leaves, celery seed, lemon verbena, and just a hint of saffron (tasty on greens) to improve your psychic energies. Along the same lines, herbal vinegars are not only tasty but eye-pleasing when made up in decorative containers. For your mental health, blend rosemary and orange in white vinegar!

In all of these cases, remember to think about the meaning of what you're making. Also consider adding in all the other sensual cues the wild woman enjoys, which also support your magick.

And what of toppings? Sauces, relishes, and other garnishes are the crowning glory of your dish so make sure they are infused with savory, scintillating magick as well!

Garnishing Ideas

Garnishing offers another imaginative way to make food meaningful. People often "eat" with their eyes first, so the more magickal your food looks, the better. Here are some suggestions:

- Use thinly shaved carrots shaped into a rose for "vision in relationships."
- Fill eggs or celery using a star-tipped pastry bag for that minipentagram effect.
- Freeze small rosebuds in ice cubes to cool the advances of a lover.
- Mold butter in cookie molds that reflect your goals.
- Cut the tops of green onions thinly—this creates a broomlike effect that sweeps away negativity.
- Use a cored pineapple as a serving dish for fruit salad to serve up heaping hospitality!

Abundance Chutney

Since berries are one of Earth's most plentiful foods, we're symbolically bringing bits of Earth's bounty to inspire our own abundance. The sweetness in this recipe makes your prosperity sweet once it arrives.

3 cups wine vinegar
½ tablespoon lemon peel, finely ground
½ tablespoon orange peel, finely ground
¼ cup diced candied ginger
1 fresh chili pepper, minced

1 clove of garlic, chopped
1 teaspoon salt
1½ cups brown sugar
3 cups mixed fresh berries
Short ¼ cup almonds or other nuts

1. Begin by lighting a candle (gold is a good color choice because it symbolizes abundance, prosperity, blessings and "all good things"). Also burn some incense that's connected to the type of abundance you most need. Leave the candle and incense burning while you prepare the recipe.

2. Boil the vinegar over a low flame.

3. Add to this the lemon and orange peels, ginger, chili pepper, garlic, and salt. Simmer for 12 to 15 minutes.

4. Stir in the brown sugar, fruit, and nuts. Simmer, stirring periodically until the mixture gets very thick and sticky (about an hour). Consider adding a chant such as this one:

> Stirred around, and around
> Abundance surrounds!

This makes about 4 cups of chutney that can be canned or used within the next few days. Tip: Let it sit overnight to enhance the flavor—and the magick.

Sassy Snacks and Appetizers

The prelude to a meal is akin to the prelude to a ritual. Both put you in the right mental and spiritual place for all that's still ahead.

In choosing your appetizers and snacks, take a moment to consider if the item matches your goal physically as well as metaphysically. For example, if your whole meal focuses on health, it makes sense to choose base components that are "healthy" (as opposed to junk food). Similarly, if your meal is intended to produce steady change, you'll want to make the appetizers and snacks from scratch as opposed to "fast food" (lasting change is rarely fast!). Here are some ideas to give you functional examples:

- Cup-size servings of French onion soup to create a protective environment
- A light salad with a predominant color matching your goals (for example, a tomato-and-red-pepper salad for love and passion)
- Pineapple and melon sliced into smiles that welcome your guests with hospitality
- Biscuits baked into cookie cutters or other symbolic forms served with herb butter

Finally, remember that appetizers shouldn't be overly heavy. I like to make just a few of them so that everyone has room for the rest of the magickal menu! Here are two recipes you can try.

Gypsy Dewdrops

When you want to break out of a rut and really kick up your heels, this recipe is ideal to turn around negativity and improve your outlook. The melon here protects you from falling into old, dull habits, and the rosemary sauce inspires the conscious mind with fresh, exciting ideas.

Serves 4

½ cup water
½ cup white wine
½ cup sugar
3" strip of orange zest
1 tablespoon chopped fresh rosemary leaves
Rosemary sprigs for garnish
¼ cup fresh orange juice
4 cups melon balls cut from a honeydew melon, chilled

1. In a small saucepan, stir together the water, the wine, the sugar, the zest, and the chopped rosemary.

2. Boil the mixture, stirring counterclockwise to decrease the influence old habits have over you.

3. Continue until the sugar is dissolved, and simmer it for 4 minutes.

4. Strain the syrup through a fine sieve set over a bowl, pressing hard on the solids, and chill it, covered, until cold.

5. Stir the orange juice into the syrup.

6. Using a serving bowl, toss the melon balls with the syrup, and garnish the dessert with the rosemary sprigs.

Gypsy Dewdrops (continued)

When you're trying to change patterns, the traditional custom has been to turn something around. For example, gamblers would turn their chairs around and sit backward to reverse bad luck. To prepare for this recipe, you can try something similar like turning your shirt inside out before starting the dish. As you turn the item of clothing, add an incantation:

> "Turn and change, turn and change—
> old ways now rearrange!"

You can continue the incantation while you cook. To make yourself more sociable and amenable to company, substitute pineapple juice, which symbolizes hospitality, for the orange juice. Likewise, to transform the way you behave in relationships, use strawberry juice; strawberries are associated with loving energy.

Bring Home the Bacon Muffins

These tasty muffins are perfect for the busy wild woman. The bacon inspires prosperity, while the baking powder and heat of the oven leaven that energy to perfection.

6 slices bacon	½ teaspoon salt
1½ cups all-purpose flour	⅓ cup finely chopped scallion
2 teaspoons baking powder	¾ cup milk
1½ teaspoons sugar	1 large egg

1. Preheat oven to 425°F and butter twelve standard-size (⅓-cup) muffin tins.

2. In a skillet, cook the bacon over moderately low heat until crisp and transfer to paper towels to drain, reserving ¼ cup bacon fat. Crumble the bacon.

3. Next, in a bowl whisk together the flour, baking powder, sugar, salt, scallion, and bacon.

4. In a small bowl whisk together milk, egg, and reserved bacon fat. Add all but a tablespoon full of this milk mixture to the flour mixture, stirring until just combined. Be careful not to overmix.

5. Divide batter evenly among muffin tins and bake in the middle of the oven for 15 minutes.

6. Take a small paintbrush and apply dollar signs with the milk mixture to the top of each muffin while saying:

" In each magick lies, Prosperity RISE! "

7. Cook for 5 more minutes until golden and a tester comes out clean. You may want to freeze a couple, too.

Beverage Bliss

Throughout the ancient world, all manner of beverages appeared on altars as offering or libations for the gods. From milk and wine to beer and water, the ancients honored beverages as a sacred thing that could rejoice the hearts of mortals and the Divine alike. I see no reason that wild women need not follow that example, especially since liquids are necessary to our bodies (for example, we have to drink lots of water anyway, so why not multitask with magick!).

Now, don't worry. You don't have to be a master brewer or a great cook to use beverages for your wild witchery. Remember that at least one of our rules is that simple = sublime (not to mention it's a timesaver!). In the setting of your sacred pantry, orange juice can be used for relationship magick, while chicken broth becomes a perfect component for health spells.

The beauty of modern living is that we have so many more options available to us now. I've seen everything from pomegranate juice to vegetable blends in the market, all of which have potential symbolic value based on the key ingredients. Get creative!

One of the handiest items in your kitchen may be the sports bottle. Since wild women are often on the go, you can make a variety of thematic beverages and then bottle them up for enjoying on the bus, while you walk, or anywhere else in your travels.

Merry Mead

Strawberries are among the sacred fruits of Freya, the Norse goddess of love and beauty, because they represented Earth's bounty. Strawberries inspire gentle, friendly love and joy with their pink-red hue. Mead was among the favorite drinks of all Teutonic peoples and is perfect for inspiring the muse when you wish to speak to your mate with sweet words.

1 pound frozen strawberries in juice
1 (16-ounce) can frozen strawberry daiquiri juice concentrate
1 gallon water
1 quart heather honey (or orange blossom, which inspires devotion)
1 orange, sliced
1 orange-flavored teabag
½ package champagne yeast

1. Place all your ingredients but the yeast in a nonaluminum pan on a medium heat.

2. Allow the mead to come to a low rolling boil.

3. As it does, some scum from the honey will rise to the top. Skim this off while reciting an incantation:

> Freya, goddess of love so sweet
> Aid my quest—make love complete
> And upon my lips warm, gentle words
> Let this prayer and need be heard.

Merry Mead (continued)

4. Continue this way for 1 hour; then let the mead cool to lukewarm. Meanwhile, place the yeast in ¼ cup of warm (*not* hot) water and stir. Let this sit until the mead has cooled properly.

5. Strain out the berries, teabag, and oranges; then blend the yeast mixture into the mead. Cover the pot with a heavy towel to work for one week (you'll know all is well if bubbles have formed on the surface within 24 hours).

6. Strain again, pouring the clearest liquid into bottles that are lightly corked and kept in a cool, dark room for two months. After this you can pour off the clearest liquid one last time, and bottle with tight-fitting corks. Allow this to age for a full year and a day before serving.

Tip: If you do not have time to age this mix, simply decrease the amount of honey to a personally pleasing level, and delete the yeast to make a nonalcoholic beverage that's good warm or cold.

Consider making this blend when the Moon is in the waxing to full phase so the mead ages properly, and so your love and happiness "waxes" likewise full! Share this at weddings, anniversaries, engagements, or romantic interludes for warm results. Especially effective if served from one common cup to symbolize unity of mind and heart.

Barbeque: The Fire Festival

The first grilling experience probably happened when a caveperson accidentally dropped food in the community fire and found out it tasted good that way. Technically speaking, barbecuing is cooking food over wood or coals (not gas!) at a low temperature for an extended time. And while there have been all manner of foods cooked in this way, barbecue as we know it probably began in the Wild West (how apt for the wild woman!). The cowhands were fed lesser cuts of meat, often heavily seasoned and left over the coals while the work was completed.

Grilling at home is a time to celebrate kinship and culinary creativity. It's an experience that begs to be shared. Maybe it's gathering under an open sky that gives us a sense of oneness with our ancestors and how they must have felt huddled around that community fire for warmth, fellowship, and, of course, dinner! Like people of old, many wild women find themselves drawn to the welcoming light, heat, and tempting smells of a fire, as well as relishing the chance to be outdoors (especially if they live in a variable season environment). Here are some ways to focus the energy to enjoy the time even more.

Plum Dandy Grilling Sauce

The word plum means "excellent" or "desirable." This sauce is designed with that meaning in mind—adding ginger for energy, sugar for life's sweetness, and clove to keep things a little spicy!

Yield: 1 cup

4 ripe red plums, cut into 1" chunks
1 tablespoon finely grated, peeled fresh gingerroot or candied ginger
1 garlic clove, diced
2 tablespoons firmly packed brown sugar
2 tablespoons water
1 tablespoon soy sauce
¼ teaspoon Chinese 5-spice blend
1 tablespoon sake (rice wine)
2 tablespoons vinegar, more if you find sauce too sweet
2 scallions, chopped

1. In a saucepan, simmer all ingredients except the vinegar and scallions, covered, stirring occasionally, until plums are falling apart, about 20 minutes.

2. Add vinegar and simmer, uncovered, stirring frequently, about 10 minutes.

3. Discard anise seeds and stir in scallions. As you apply this sauce to your meat on the grill, add an incantation:

> " Plums to raise desire higher
> Ginger for energy on the open fire
> Sugar that life may be ever sweet
> Magick saturate this blessed meat! "

Ribs for Richness

Prepare these ribs and watch finances improve! In the Celtic vision of heaven, there is a sow that never ceases to yield meat and feed the hungry. Thus those who are lucky enough to enter paradise partake of pork for eternity. In modern-day tradition, pork is believed to be good-luck food that protects wealth and longevity. To this symbolism, we add honey for sweet success, and ginger for energy to create magick.

Serves 4

2 sides baby back pork ribs
½ cup soy or teriyaki sauce
1 cup orange juice
⅓ cup orange rum (or vodka)
½ cup apple juice
¼ cup honey
1 teaspoon powdered ginger
1 teaspoon orange zest
½ cup minced chives or green onions
2 tablespoons minced garlic

1. The first step of this dish starts indoors. Fill a large pan with about ½" of water. Place a cookie grill or something similar across the top of the pan and arrange the ribs on the grill. The water in the pan will provide insulation from the direct heat and keep the ribs moist while cooking.

2. Cover with aluminum foil and cook at 250° until the meat begins to retract from the bones.

Ribs for Richness (continued)

3. Meanwhile, in another pan, combine the remaining ingredients and stir over a low flame so the honey is evenly mixed in.

Stir this clockwise saying:

> Honey, make my life complete
> Ginger, my prosperity will be fast and sweet
> Apple and orange, blessings bestow
> Manifested by fire, as above so below!

4. Pour all but about 1 cup of this mixture over the cooked ribs, marinating them in the refrigerator for about 2 to 3 hours so they absorb the flavor and energy.

5. Prepare your grill by brushing it with a little cooking oil so the ribs won't stick. Wait until the grill has a nice medium flame (about 320°).

6. Cook the ribs, turning them once every 5 minutes; turn the ribs four times to make sure they are cooked and marinated thoroughly.

7. Brush with the remaining marinade at each turn.

In the United States we often equate money with the color green, so decorate your sacred space with lots of green highlights (gold is also a good alternative for prosperity). You can also use oriental paper lanterns in appropriate symbolic colors; they work beautifully outside near the barbeque and add a nice ambiance.

Mystical Meat and Fish

Meat or fish are typically the centerpiece of major meals. They are the main course, creating a theme around which all other dishes and beverages are usually planned. Metaphysically speaking, beef has associations with providence, prosperity, and grounding; chicken with well-being; and fish with abundance, fertility, and miracles. Here are some sample dishes.

Decision Chicken

If you're in a quandary, whip up this tasty dish. Chicken and mustard guide fact-finding, so you'll have the best information necessary to make a good decision. The maple syrup (or honey) ensures that your choice makes you truly happy.

1 good-size boneless chicken breast
1/4 cup cider vinegar
1/4 cup sesame oil
2 tablespoons soy sauce
1 teaspoon salt
1 teaspoon ginger

2 tablespoons brown sugar
2 slices orange
1/4 cup cooking wine
1/8 cup coarse-ground honey mustard
1/4 cup maple syrup or orange blossom honey
Pat of butter

1. Pierce the chicken with a fork while holding the thought of breaking through any illusions or misconceptions that you may be working on releasing.

2. Marinate chicken in a blend of the vinegar, oil, soy, salt, ginger, brown sugar, and the juice of two orange slices.

3. Let the meat soak in the refrigerator for 6 hours, turning it regularly saying something like:

> A choice to make, magick be my guide
> Quickly and correctly, help me decide!

4. Create the glaze by mixing the wine, mustard, maple syrup or honey, and butter in a saucepan.

5. Brush this on the chicken as you bake it, turning every 7 to 8 minutes (about four times total).

Consider cooking at "in-between" times like noon or dawn. This encourages balanced perspectives.

Babble Fish

This dish accents creative communications, especially with those ever-annoying know-it-alls, wiseacres, gossips, conversation hogs, and those who are quick to jump into discussions just to hear themselves talk! The yellow parsnips, carrots, and pepper reflect the air element, which empowers our words.

2 medium carrots
2 medium parsnips
1 yellow pepper (large)
2 tablespoons butter
2 cups sliced cabbage
1 tablespoon white vinegar
¾ cup soy sauce
4 (4–5 ounce) fish fillets
Olive oil
¾ pound sweet potato, peeled and cooked tender

　　1. Cut carrots, parsnips, and yellow pepper into thin strips. As you do, focus on "cutting through" anything that stands between you and speaking your mind.

　　2. In a large frying pan (indoors or on the side burner of your grill), place the butter, carrots, pepper, and parsnips to fry. As you notice the carrots and parsnips getting tender, add the cabbage into the fray, along with the vinegar and soy sauce.

Babble Fish (continued)

3. Coat the vegetables evenly (you want the magick to flow evenly into all the components) while saying:

> Parsnips, help me speak my mind
> With carrots and cabbage, my magick binds
> Potatoes put me on firm ground
> Creative communications shall abound!

4. When the vegetables are close to being fully cooked, place the fish into a no-stick frying pan with just a touch of olive oil and cook over a low heat.

5. Using a knife, or toothpick if the fish is delicate, carve a symbol into the fillet that represents your goal.

6. Brown the fish about 5 minutes on each side, adjusting for thickness.

7. Serve the fish on the bed of sweet potatoes, which will create a firm foundation for your spell. Since fish are symbolically associated with abundance, this dish makes sure you're never at a loss for words!

Enjoy a piece of mint candy or gargle with mouthwash before working this spell. Since you want to manifest the best possible communications, this emphasizes the goal from the inside out. Additionally, mint supports effective interactions.

Vegetarian Fare

A vegetarian diet is nothing new. Pythagoras, who lived around 560 B.C., is often called the father of vegetarianism since he felt that eating meat could cause a kind of trauma (because the spirit of the animal experienced trauma). His followers adhered to the vegetarian lifestyle quite diligently. Other famous vegetarians include Louisa May Alcott (author of *Little Women*) and Clara Barton (who founded the American Red Cross).

Out of respect for nature, some wild women have chosen to become vegetarians. For those who have, the extra benefits are twofold. First, you can grow a fair variety of vegetables with little space, thus allowing you to plant and harvest by the Moon's cycles to energize them. Second, vegetables, grains, and other vegetarian fare don't dull energy as heavier meats do. The exception to this rule comes in the form of root vegetables, which reconnect us to the earth in a strong way. Here's one recipe for you to try:

Outrageous, Courageous Rice

This recipe originates in Greco-Roman tradition where it was considered simple fare. We derive the symbolic value of this dish from the red peppers that provide zest, and from the traditional regional symbolism for borage—namely, courage, strength of character, and improved outlook. In relationships, apply this energy when you're trying something new in the bedroom or when you're feeling ethically uncertain about a passionate situation.

3 cups water	1 red pepper, sliced thinly
1½ cups of rice	½ green pepper, sliced thinly
2 teaspoons dried borage *(Borago officinalis)*	1 tablespoon olive oil

1. Place the water, rice, and borage into a pot and bring it to a low rolling boil.

2. While this is warming, sauté the pepper slices gently in oil. As you move them around the pan, visualize a reddish pink light filling them and intone:

> Courage and energy in every bite
> Grant me brave perspectives and magickal might!!

3. When the rice is boiling, cover and simmer (20 minutes) until cooked.

4. Top the rice with the sautéed peppers and enjoy.

Tip: If you'd like to add some happiness to the equation, decrease the borage by a teaspoon and replace with 1 teaspoon of marjoram.

Wild and Wonderful Desserts

Okay, I confess. This wild woman has a sweet tooth the size of Texas. There is something about desserts that seem in keeping with a wild woman's zest for experiencing life to the fullest. The sweeteners in many desserts also underscore that "sweet slice of life" everyone yearns for. Honey, in particular, offers harmony, love, joy, good communication, and creativity.

In history, desserts were as much decorative and playful as they were sweet treats. Part of their function was to mirror the feeling of the whole meal, even in their appearance. They were even used in mischief—in the nursery rhyme "Sing a Song of Sixpence," birds were hidden in a piecrust as a surprise. This amusing and symbolic application for desserts makes them perfect for wild women. In this case, we can truly have our cake and eat it too!

Here are a couple of desserts to consider adding to your magickal menus.

Inventive Grapes

When you want to find a creative way of coping with difficult issues, try this treat and nibble away at some calm resourcefulness. Use green grapes for monetary or mundane issues, red grapes for emotional issues, and purple grapes for spiritual issues. The walnuts in this recipe accent your ability to think clearly.

3 ounces softened cream cheese
1 tablespoon crystallized ginger, finely chopped
½ teaspoon orange juice
15–20 seedless grapes (large)
¼ cup finely powdered walnuts

1. Blend the cream cheese with the ginger and orange juice, using a hand blender to "whip up" the energy.

2. Roll each of the grapes in this mixture, turning them clockwise to coat them evenly saying:

> Round and round the magick wraps
> Improve my creativity, help me adapt!

3. Chill them in the freezer for 10 minutes.

4. Meanwhile, pour the walnuts onto a piece of waxed paper. Roll the grapes into this powder again so they're evenly coated. Chill again to likewise chill out your emotions!

Heart-Pleasing Hazelnut Pudding

Prepare this pudding any time you want to smooth out a bumpy relationship, or spice up a good one!

Serves 4

½ cup hazelnuts (about 2 ounces), toasted and husked
5 tablespoons sugar
4 ounces semisweet chocolate, chopped
3 large eggs, separated

5 tablespoons water
2 tablespoons brandy or vanilla flavoring
Pinch of salt
½ cup chilled whipping cream

1. Light a vibrant red candle to set the mood, and say:

> With good intention, by my will
> With the power of love, this pudding fill
> Nuts for wisdom and feelings sweet
> My magick fills this little treat!

2. Grind hazelnuts with 1 tablespoon sugar in processor until mixture forms paste.

3. Melt chocolate in small metal bowl set over a saucepan of simmering water, stirring until smooth.

4. Remove the bowl from the water. As you do, visualize any problems between you and your mate likewise melting away, leaving nothing but warm sweetness.

5. Whisk egg yolks, 2 tablespoons water, brandy or vanilla flavoring, and 2 tablespoons sugar in a large metal bowl to blend. Focus intently on your feelings and try to remember always to stir clockwise to keep that warm, welcoming energy moving forward.

Heart-Pleasing Hazelnut Pudding (continued)

6. Set the bowl over the same saucepan of simmering water and whisk constantly until thick ribbons form when the whisk is lifted and until a thermometer inserted into the mixture registers 160°F, about 6 minutes.

7. Cool the mixture slightly. Fold in the chocolate and hazelnut paste.

8. Using an electric mixer, beat the egg whites and pinch of salt in a large bowl until soft peaks form. Because of the upbeat energy created by the mixer, this is a good time to add an incantation:

> " Higher and higher, our hearts fill with fire
> Passion and love, blessed from above! "

9. Visualize the whites being filled with a sparkling pink light (pink being the color of gentle love). Stir the remaining 2 tablespoons sugar and 3 tablespoons water into a very small saucepan over medium heat until the sugar dissolves.

10. Increase the heat and boil the syrup until a thermometer inserted into it registers 220°F, about 4 minutes.

11. Gradually add the hot syrup to the egg whites, beating until firm peaks form and the whites are cool. Fold into the chocolate mixture in two additions.

12. Beat the whipping cream in a medium bowl until soft peaks form. Fold into the mousse.

13. Spoon the mousse into four goblets, dividing equally. Chill for at least 1 hour and up to 1 day. Garnish each serving with whipped cream and toasted hazelnuts.

I realize that many wild women don't have a lot of time for fussing. If you're in that category, do not despair. Even prepared foods can become spiritually energized. Choose them thoughtfully—for the symbolism of the ingredients. For example, if mac and cheese is your ultimate comfort food, eat it when you need comforting energy! And don't forget to pray or intone over it before serving.

Summary

The wild woman knows that if she's stressed out by magick, it's not going to work. What is most important is to have the process be both comfortable and meaningful. So, stick to simple and sublime, and trust yourself and your instincts. Everything else, as they say, is icing on the cake!

five

The Gypsy Woman

Wild Nights—Wild Nights!
Were I with thee
Wild Nights should be, Our luxury!
—Emily Dickinson

n looking at history, one of the wonderful examples of wild women comes from the Gypsy tradition. These ladies loved being women, they loved the insights being a woman afforded, and they used their feminine, intuitive wiles to their benefit, often putting unwary visitors at a huge disadvantage! Among the many Gypsy talents, one in particular shines through, that of being a seer and diviner.

Many people think of divination as only revealing the future, but both Gypsies and wild women know better. The traditional "seer" was part priestess and part counselor. While most people are naturally curious about their future, they have a far greater need for insights into the here-and-now. Correspondingly, divination, in practice, tends to respond more strongly to needs versus their wants. Thus the art of fortunetelling, once learned, also provides perspectives on perplexing present concerns (even if that's not what you've asked about!).

Now, since wild women want to be in fate's driver's seat, and since focus and control are important to them, the diviner's art affords women a valuable tool when it seems as if our vision is wanting. But ours is not the world of our ancestors, and some of the methods used by the ancients seem foreign to our perceptions and hard to comprehend. With that in mind, this chapter focuses on both traditional and creative divination methods that you can test in answering all kinds of questions from love to finances and job hunting. As you find the methods that work, stick with them, personalize them, and take notes of your results so you can come back for new insights later!

Your Inner Psychic

No exploration of divination would be complete without addressing human psychic aptitude. I've always hated the phrase *supernatural ability* because it somehow implies that psychic aptitude is un-natural or above nature. However, if you look at animal instincts, or better still at intuitions that have come to pass, that's obviously not the case. Psychic aptitude is a part of human nature that has been dismissed because it can't easily be qualified or quantified.

Being a wild woman requires us to break free of unbalanced societal training that shrugs off instinctual responses and trusts logic alone. Honestly, how many times have you done that and later regretted not listening to that little voice inside? That little voice is also tied to your inner psychic! So the next obvious question becomes, how do you activate it fully?

Throughout time, seers, kings, and commoners alike have tried various methods for awakening these gifts. A fair number of these techniques are still used today to improve the flow of spiritual energy and to bring a person's conscious awareness to higher, more receptive levels. They include:

- Meditation and visualization
- Chanting, prayer, or mantras
- Cleansing and purification
- Minirituals or spells
- Relaxation and breathing

For the sake of space, I'd like to address the two simplest helpmates: physical environment and personal preparation. Look first to the area where you might enact a reading for yourself or someone else; consider if there's anything there that would distract you? For example, if the only private spot you have is your bedroom, a bunch of unsorted laundry on the bed is a huge distraction. It speaks of mundane tasks that aren't done, and it will likely deter your focus. You need to determine what distractions will hijack your mental focus and move them out of your sight.

Create an atmosphere that's speaks to all of your senses of the goal at hand. This is an ideal time to bring some calming music, candlelight, some witchy clothing, and divinatory incense into the equation. Avoid music with words because it can make communicating your insights more difficult (or, if you're writing down what you see, you can end up writing the song's words quite unwittingly).

Candlelight is less harsh than fluorescent, but make sure you have enough light to see your chosen medium clearly. As far as clothing goes, what makes you feel magickal? And, last but not least, aromas that open those psychic gateways include bay, cinnamon, honeysuckle, and mint. For prophetic energies, try jasmine or rose. For spiritual insight, stick with lotus or sandalwood.

Personal preparation before you try any divinatory system is really pretty much the same as for any metaphysical process. Make sure you're well rested, your mood is upbeat, and your health is good. Any negativity you're carrying around can easily skew the reading to make things look much worse than the reality.

In addition to these basics, I suggest washing your hands before you begin. This is a nice symbolic gesture that cleanses away any bits of stray energy you might have gathered during the day. It's also quite traditional to be clean when working with sacred implements, the implication being that you are then a pure vessel through which the energy and insights can flow.

If after trying several systems and using these suggestions, you're still having trouble with divination, try meditation, chanting, and so on. Don't be discouraged. We live in a concrete world, and divination touches on that unseen space that's hard for many people to reach. With a little tenacity, you'll eventually discover the right combination of elements that work successfully for you without much ado whatsoever.

Decisions, Decisions: Choosing a Divination System

In deciding among divination systems, first ask yourself which sense you associate with most strongly. Tactile people will naturally be more attracted to runes, stones, and similar systems that have textural quality. Visual people will enjoy things like the tarot. Auditory people might look to natural omens and signs (specifically sounds). Generally speaking, if you can find a divination system that appeals to your key sense, you'll have greater success.

Second, you must decide which symbols make sense to you. I might like the art of the Japanese Tarot, but a lot of the symbols are culturally unknown to me. I could learn them, but I'm not sure the impact for a reading would be as clear and meaningful as the Whimsical Tarot, which I use. Even if a system's appearance is appealing, other factors influence how well it may (or may not) work for you. These factors range from the creator's perspectives to the cultural influences around that particular system.

Third, you need to consider how you plan to apply the tool. If you just want yes or no answers, a nice coin minted in the year of your birth is just fine. On the other hand, if you're asking about underlying energies in a situation, yes and no answers will leave you wanting. If you are working with more detailed questions, then runes, stones, animal cards, or tarot provide more diversity of symbols—and thus more explanation.

Finally, which systems seem to appeal to your higher senses? You know you're on the right track when you look at them, hold them, or meditate about them, and they seem comfortable and welcoming. This is very important. You're not going to be able to use a tool effectively that you're ill at ease with.

With those points in mind, you can see why it's not a good idea to buy a divination system sight unseen. To resolve this issue, many New Age stores have sample packs that you can open, examine, and try on-site to ensure you're making the best choice possible. If you cannot find such a store, ask some of your wild, witchy friends if they have any systems they like that you can look at. Don't rush this choice. It's worth taking the time to find a system that truly sings the song of your soul in a meaningful way.

Winging It: Creating or Adapting Divination Systems

You've been shopping everywhere and it just seems as though each divination system you find isn't quite right. Some are too expensive. Some have symbols you can't begin to fathom. Others you like, but they still seem somehow lacking or flat. What do you do? Hey, that kind of obstacle has never stopped a wild woman before. Get adventurous! Make your own system or adapt one that's close to what you want.

If you want to make your own system, what's the first step? Decide whether you're going to base it on an existing method, or on a method wholly of your devising. For example, if you like tarot cards but can't find a deck that you enjoy, you can make a personalized set based on the traditional interpretation of the cards. In this case, you might cut out images from magazines and decoupage them onto 3" × 5" cards. That way every image in the deck is meaningful and appeals to your senses.

Step 2 is to figure out your medium. Paper? Stones? Dice? Nuts and bolts? In picking out a medium, consider durability and portability. Since the wild woman is on the go, you want something that can handle your pace (and something that's forgiving of spilled coffee!). Personally speaking, I've chosen a variety of crystals for my set, but you could also use wood slices, laminated paper, and so on.

Step 2 brings an important point to bear. There are many items around your home that could become part of your wild woman's divination system. From the magazine cutouts to trinkets in your junk drawer, everything has potential in a spiritual construct if you think about it differently. Also, those items that come from your living space are already charged with your personal energy.

Okay, step 3. Will you be laying out your system, casting it, tossing it, or drawing it? A lot of times your medium determines this for you, and some systems can be used a variety of ways. With crystals, you can draw them (pull them blindly from a bag) or cast them (toss them onto a surface)! The only caution here is that your items need to be very similar in size and shape for a drawn system. Otherwise there's a chance you could unconsciously skew a reading by recognizing one item from the others as you pull them out of their container.

Step 4 is deciding if you want to include negative (or reversed) meanings. With card-oriented systems this is fairly easy to do, but with cast systems it gets tricky. In that case, if you want symbolism that talks about obstacles or other negatives, set it up as a specific space on the casting surface.

Step 5 gets interesting. Now's the time to determine the meaning behind each of the items you've included in your set depending on the order in which you pull them, or where they land on the casting surface. For example, in my crystal set, amethyst typically represents self-control. If it lands in the western part of the casting cloth, the additional symbolism is that of emotional impact (i.e., needing to be aware of and in control of how feelings affect me).

Last but not least, in step 6, try the system out. This is when you typically discover any little bugs, like its not having enough components for detailed readings. Normally I suggest a system have no fewer than thirteen symbols to allow for diversity. Adjust the system to fix the problems you find; then start using it!

Making a personal divination system is a bit time-consuming. Some wild women might feel a bit overwhelmed trying to add this into an already busy schedule. If that's the case, you could simply adapt a pre-existing system to your needs. The process is somewhat similar, but in this case you're jumping to step 6 and determining what you don't like about the prefabricated method, and how you could fix it. For example, if you're not fond of the suggested layouts for a card-oriented system, create your own layouts. Or, if a few of the stones in a crystal oracle don't speak to you, replace them with others that do!

While I hope that you find the ideal system without having to go through all these steps, I'm realistic. Wild women do not like to settle for second best, nor should they have to, and that applies to divination tools, too! Anything that you utilize for your spiritual well-being should be special, and "just right." The closer it's honed to your vision, the better the results will be.

Reading for Yourself and Others

There are some good rules of thumb when you're working with divination tools that encourage the greatest amount of success. The first is to be well rested and in a good state of mind. When you're tired or pissed off, it's bound to be reflected in the reading and can skew your interpretation.

Second, make sure you won't be interrupted during the reading. Often insights into the way the symbols work together come as you move into a focused state during the reading. If the phone is ringing, the dog's barking, or whatever—you may miss important messages.

Third, bring as many of your senses into the process as possible. Accomplish this by adding candlelight, aromatics, music, and other touches that help set the mood.

Fourth, when reading for others, make sure you can set aside any personal knowledge of the person's situation, or any bad feelings you may harbor toward the person. If you can't—politely decline the reading. If you can, try to avoid looking for information in the reading that isn't there. No matter what the question may be, there can be something else on which Spirit wants him or her to focus. You need to trust yourself, your inner psychic, and your tools.

Last, but not least, try to be a positive prophet for yourself and others. There are good ways to communicate bad news, especially when you remember that having a feel for the underlying energies today, or what's just ahead, can help us turn that negative around. The information derived from divination is meant to be a helpmate *only*; it is not carved into stone. Use it to gain perspectives. Use it to become more proactive. Use it to prepare for the future, but wild women don't let this (or anything else) become a crutch.

Original Oracles

Now that you have all the information for choosing your divinatory tool, let's look at some creative media that you can use when you've forgotten your normal divination set or when you'd like to try something new.

It's Okay to Play with Your Food

Well, I am a kitchen witch, so sometimes I *do* play with my food for divinatory purposes. For example, I'll scry the surface of my creamer with a question in mind and watch for images to appear—much as I might observe the surface of a crystal ball, or the movements of a candle flame. What's kind of neat is that using food items in divination is actually a very old art. Priestesses of Apollo sprinkled flour on water and scried the images, Victorians peeled and tossed apple skins looking for initials to form, Romans observed curdling milk for patterns, Greeks looked at spattered wine, and reading tea leaves began in sixth-century China! The beauty of divining with food is actually threefold. First, you can prepare dishes with ingredients that symbolize your question to energize the process. Second, there are a huge variety of potential media from which to choose. Third, you can eat the results of positive readings to internalize that energy, thus giving whole new meaning to "you are what you eat!"

Here are a couple of examples:

Mashed potatoes: Think of a question while you stir the potatoes on your plate. Don't look directly at them. Rather unfocus your eyes a bit and see if you've drawn any identifiable images in the surface (or if the whole surface looks like something). You can use nearly any symbol book to interpret the value for the image if the meaning isn't immediately obvious. This approach works with anything that's got a smooth texture, including icing and thick gravy.

Alphabet soup: Focus on your question while you're eating. When you get close to the bottom of the bowl, see what letters remain and if they spell something (or perhaps make up someone's initials).

Spills: Next time you spill milk, don't cry over it—scry it! Liquids aren't the only medium this approach works with either. A bit of flour, coffee grounds, spices, or sugar on the countertop may reveal patterns.

Bean casting: Beans come in a wonderful variety of colors, which provides some built-in interpretive value. Scatter them on a square surface. Those that land in the east reveal something about your communication, the south speaks to your energy levels, the west to your emotions, while the north represents mundane and financial matters. So, if a red bean were to land in the south, you might ask yourself if you're giving too much energy to a love interest (the south represents your energy levels while red is the color of love or passion).

If you take a minute to look around your kitchen and pantry I'm sure you'll find more options just waiting for your wild whimsy!

Book It

If you've ever thought of a question and then randomly opened a book and sought out the first line you see as the answer, you've practiced the time-honored art of bibliomancy. Traditionally this was enacted with the

Bible or a person's favorite literary masterpiece. However, you can use whatever book is available—from cookbooks to the telephone directory.

Additionally, consider the ways in which technology has advanced from our ancestors' time and use that to your advantage. We now have books on tape, books on video, and books on CDs! These media can be used just like the book except that you fast-forward the tape, video, or CD/DVD while you're thinking of your question, and then listen to the answer you get!

Another way to apply this concept is on your computer. Go to your favorite search engine and type in a word or phrase that embodies your question. Close your eyes and focus intently on that question while keeping your hands in contact with the mouse and keyboard. Now, click and see what search results you get. At random, go to a predetermined number of sites (such as four for earth/money matters); then look to the first phrase you see there (or even a whole article) that gives you insights.

Getting Carded

Cartomancy, or the art of divination by cards, is perhaps the most popular form of fortunetelling in the New Age. There are literally hundreds of tarot decks from which the wild woman could choose. But what happens when none seem to fit the bill? That's when you hunker down and get creative!

There are several solutions to the tarot issue. The first is a plain set of playing cards. Here, spades relate to various challenges and obstacles, clubs are business or pragmatic matters, hearts are emotional issues, and diamonds deal with money. There are some "traditionally" ascribed meanings to each card, but I see no reason not to make up your own, perhaps based on numerology. For example, the two of hearts might portend a beneficial relationship with romantic potential.

If you're not familiar with numerology, don't worry! There are at least three more options to consider. What about a greeting-card tarot? You can collect the covers, the messages, or both from various cards you get from family and friends. The meaningfulness of each card is augmented by the good wishes of the sender. Each card will typically have an obvious meaning that you can translate into a layout. For example, a "get well" card that turns up in an "underlying circumstances" position might be a gentle counsel to check your health, or that your health is somehow influencing the question at hand.

The two other options that immediately come to mind are creating a coupon deck or perhaps one from business cards. Since these aren't quite as sturdy as other media, you may want to laminate them. Alternatively, use the coupons or give out the business cards when you're done with a reading to spread the energy around!

How would you go about determining the meanings of coupons or business cards? With coupons, consider the product's name or function. For example Joy dish detergent would apply to your happiness in the reading. Or, a coupon for bandages might apply to an area of your life that needs comfort or healing. With business cards, try considering the function of the company or its name, like a plumbing company symbolizing things that are "stopped up" or "blocked" in your life.

The Office Oracle

If you're already working with business cards as makeshift divination tools, it's only a hop, skip, and a jump away from using other everyday business items. Paper clips, staples, glue sticks, pen caps, labels, binder clips, filing cabinet keys, stamps, paper reinforcers, and other small items can easily become part of a cast system. As with cartomancy, you'll develop the meaning of each item by its immediate symbolic value to you (and its normal function). For example, paper clips talk about loose connections, pen caps deal with communications, keys represent openings and closings (or safety), and binder clips gather large groupings into one spot, offering security.

Bearing in mind that each person's "office" is different, you'll probably find a lot of unique things that reflect not only who you are and what you do but also offer great symbolic value. For example, a woodworker's list might consist of things such as screws, nuts, nails, tacks, wood glue, and so forth. Make a list of these items; then write down the meanings alongside each item. Finally, ask yourself how those meanings will change depending on how each item lands in the casting.

Toy Time

Sometimes it may seem hard to be a wild woman when you've got children. Just when you're ready to kick up your heels, they want your attention. That's perfectly normal, but children are very magickal in their own right, as are many of the things with which they play. Harry Potter toys and books come immediately to mind as a great example. So when you start getting a little frustrated by having to clean up all kinds of small tokens, dollhouse props, dominoes, and game pieces, take two steps back and think about how they could be used in divination.

Dominoes already have a system that's technically called cleromancy. To try this, put the whole set face-down on a table and choose one at random. The number combination you get provides the interpretive value. Double six means luck, for example, whereas a double four (Earth-oriented) means financial improvements. Any book on numerology can give you more ideas along these lines.

Tokens, props, and pieces also make for a fun cast system. Put them into a sand bucket, shake them up, and release them to a casting surface. Anything that lands off that surface isn't used in the interpretation. The items that land within the casting surface can be interpreted similarly to the other cast systems in this chapter. For example, a dollhouse lamp that lands in the southern part of a surface could be interpreted as either burning your candle too brightly or the need to shine a light (a focus) on your energy levels. The automobile token from Monopoly that lands in the east portends an adventurous trip (the vehicle combines with the movement of the air element).

Just remember to put everything back when you're done or the kids will call you on it, trust me!

Summary

As you can see, nearly anything can become a useful and functional divination system if you apply a bit of your wild wit and wisdom to the process. About the only caution is to remember that once you decide to use something as a magickal tool, treat it as such. The respect and mental attitude with which you approach any reading method makes a great deal of difference in its outcome.

Six

Wild Relationships
and Sexy Sorcery

Dearest dealer,
I with my royal straight flush,
love you so for your wild card,
that untamable, eternal, gut-driven,
ha-ha, and lucky love.
—Anne Sexton

ild women do everything fully. They love fully; they give passion fully. They are tried-and-true friends and aren't afraid of positively expressing their feelings, needs, or sexuality to suit the circumstances. Mind you, all this openness and confidence doesn't happen overnight. In fact, many women have to do a lot of healing and adjusting to reach a place where wild relationships become possible without guilt and without painful memories haunting their reality. With that in mind, why not use a little magick to help things along when you suddenly start slipping into negativity, old habits, and unproductive relationship patterns?

Before launching into the how-to's of relationship magick, there is a brief caveat known to the wisest of wild women. Quite simply, relationships should not be manipulated. If you want friendships, lovers, or marriages that are truly meaningful, you also want to know they came honestly—not because of a love spell or potion! Ethically speaking, that means your magick must be designed to open the way for good relationships, rather than trying to control another's intent or feelings.

Wild women are so goal driven and passionate that this can often be a point of resistance for them. However, it is easier than you think; it is simply a matter of releasing and acceptance. You must first release your desire to "hold" a specific person or persons to you, thereby honoring their individuality and independence. Then you can go on to accept and integrate free will as an essential factor in planning the magickal process. The activities in this chapter provide some ideas when fashioning your own nonmanipulative relationship magick.

Social Sizzle

Humans are tribal creatures. Put simply, we need other people to maintain mental well-being. Socialization is one of the keys to our development as children; it's a way that we learn about the world and how we get a lot of valuable "hard-knock" lessons. Friendships reveal what types of people and personalities will nurture our strengths, talents, and inner wild woman. Relationships are also a mirror of our personality. For example, if you are surrounded by wonderful and generous people, then you will have enough self-esteem to recognize those qualities in yourself. If your relationships leave something to be desired, then allow that to be a catalyst for soul-searching and inner work.

A wild woman doesn't normally allow herself to become the proverbial wallflower in life's dance. Rather, she realizes that getting out there, kicking up her heels, and mingling is good for her; it celebrates the wild within. Conversely, wild women also know when to back off a bit from the social scene. If we sit out a song or two, it's because we simply need privacy, downtime, and time to replenish our most important relationship—the one with ourselves. So as you go through this chapter, please keep balance in mind. When you need "you" time—take it! When you need to be with other people and socialize—*dance!*

The Dance of Life

> Let us whirl like a compass around the point of Divine Grace.   —Rumi

Among the Sufi, dance is a form of moving meditation through which the individual, or group, seeks unity and ecstasy. Overall, the purpose of the dance is to relinquish a sense of separateness and come to a fullness of being within and without. Sacred dance can have many goals, but here, you can use it as a means of celebrating the self and uplifting your spirit before you go into a social situation. This way, the person you present shines with magick; unlike a plastic façade, this energy is genuine and radiates from within. It's irresistible!

Sacred dance need not have any particular movements, but one of the most popular is moving slowly in a circle. Here you become the point of a beautiful mandala, where your spirit moves both inward and upward to reach the Divine Self. Begin by taking time to move things in the room where you want to dance so you won't trip over anything and can safely close your eyes. You can also burn a little sandalwood incense to cleanse the space and create a foundation of spirituality.

Next, close your eyes, and listen closely to your breathing and your heartbeat. That is your own personal rhythm. It beats out a code that's yours alone. Wrap your arms around yourself and gently sway to that beat. Move in whatever way you feel (there is no right or wrong here). Just *be* in the moment. As you sway, visualize your unique essence or energy as a glowing flame centered in your heart—warm, vibrant, and welcoming.

As you continue to dance, picture this energy radiating out from your heart center and filling your entire body and eventually your aura. Feel the energy rise until it's overflowing. Slowly stop your movement and just revel in that moment. Take that energy with you as you go into a social setting. You'll find people see you very differently and may even comment on your "glow."

BE-attitude Amulet

The wild woman knows that the most attractive quality is confidence. What some might even call "attitude." Symbolically, bees are messengers that represent mindfulness and tapping into our creative energy or inner muse. For this amulet, try to find a pin (or a key chain or something similarly small and portable) with a depiction of a bee on it. You'll also need some of your favorite perfume or aromatic oil. Dab a bit on the bee image, and then close both your hands over it. Whisper, "I am" three times, letting your voice grow in power each time. Now, what do you most need to build up in yourself? Confidence? Presence? Find one word and add that to "I am _____," repeating it again three times, focusing on your goal. Finally, wear or carry the amulet. When you most need that particular characteristic to manifest, touch the amulet and say, "Blessed be, let my spell be freed!"

However, there's more to socialization than a sense of presence and energy. Communication also plays a huge part in how effectively we socialize. A wild woman has a sharp wit and a keen tongue. She can easily wield sooth or savvy words, just as she can, in no uncertain terms, communicate her boundaries. With this in mind, what accouterments can we consider for communication fitting the wild woman persona? What about breath mints—with a pinch of magick!

Skillful Speech Mints

Start by getting a container of breath mints (any type you enjoy is fine). Place a little swatch of natural yellow cloth inside the container; yellow represents the air element, which governs communications. Set the container in natural sunlight and moonlight for three hours each so the mints are infused with energy for both logical and intuitive speech. Finally, hold the container in your hands, and visualize it being filled with a pale yellow, sparkling light and say:

> Words be clear, words be sweet
>
> My magick's in these little treats
>
> With each mint, fresh words I'll state
>
> Empowered to communicate!

Tuck them into a purse or briefcase and enjoy one whenever you find your words failing you, or just before you know you'll be in a difficult communication situation—such as an important meeting or presentation. By the way, you can choose the flavor of your candy according to specific goals. Cinnamon, for example, is excellent for passionate communication, or any discourse when you need to be psychically aware as you talk. Mint, by comparison, aids with financial and travel discussions.

Friendship

The wild woman values her close friends greatly. Whereas family has to put up with us because we live in the same house, friends choose that task, and we choose our friends! Interestingly enough, research agrees with the wild woman's outlook on friendship. People with friends generally fare better physically and mentally. Why? Because friends create a support network that provides tangible assistance, a caring ear, a common ground for pondering ideas, and someone with whom to play! In very real ways, our friends become a coping mechanism for most of life's ups and downs.

So how do you discover new friends, and more important, how do you go about staying close to the friends you already have? Much of it boils down to words you have in your vocabulary: sensitivity, honesty, consideration, and old-fashioned elbow grease. Relationships need regular maintenance, and that includes spiritual maintenance. That's where your magick comes in!

Tea for Two (or More)

The next time you get together with one or more friends, how about making a special witch's brew that decreases any lingering stress, provides gentle comfort, and facilitates rapport? I suggest blending 1 cup of water per person with lemon peel (friendship), one strand of saffron (joy and well-being), a pinch of nutmeg (devotion), and black teabags (energy). Focus on your goal of oneness as you create the blend, and serve it garnished with a violet flower or sprig of lavender to accent harmony.

Listening Charm

Perhaps the most important part of any friendship is being able to establish a balance of give-and-take. The wild woman knows that friendships, or any relationship for that matter, will falter if energy is not recycled. Listening is a difficult art to master; it requires learning how other people communicate, and understanding what they are really saying. The wild woman knows that she has to listen with her intuition as well as her ears. Every time you interact with a new person it is, in effect, like learning a new language!

This charm is intended to help you hone your listening skills. It begins with an earring (or a pair of earrings). At one time, lore indicated that the ear was pierced and given a decoration to remind us not to eavesdrop! That's not a bad idea for the wild woman either, but you can go one step further in blessing and charging this token for your goal. If possible, it's best to use a gold earring, a color that symbolizes awareness and good communication skills. You'll want to let the earring charge in sunlight to accent the conscious/awake mind. You also should place it in moonlight as well, so that as you listen, you can hear the meaning behind a person's words. Finally, add an incantation just before you put the earring on like:

> When to listen, when to speak
>
> Wisdom in both is what I seek
>
> And when words come to my ear
>
> Only true intention shall I hear.

When you notice your attention wandering in a conversation, or you feel as though you're not getting the real message, touch your earring and mentally recite your incantation again to support the magick.

Dating

Dating is an activity that practically begs for sexy sorcery. You may have found one, or several, partners you want to spend more time with on a regular basis. This is certainly a situation in which magick can help. It's also one in which your wild woman's wisdom will come in handy. It's easy to let dormant insecurities and jealous naysayers blow potential relationships, but a wild woman can employ some sound psychological strategies in combination with her metaphysical efforts. These include:

- **Realize that not everyone is your soul mate, and not everyone is a nerd or "user."** Make no assumptions, and maintain realistic expectations. If you go into a relationship with a negative attitude or unreasonable hopes, it's certain *not* to work out.
- **Accentuate the positive.** This doesn't mean hiding any bad habits, because time reveals all truths. If you're meant to be with this person for more than a fling, he or she won't mind discovering how you look before coffee!
- **Take off the rose-colored glasses.** If this person's values, lifestyle, or beliefs don't mesh with yours, it's doubtful that love will "conquer all" any time in the future. If you just want a little fun—go for it! Just don't collapse yourself into a go-nowhere relationship.

- **Avoid drama**. Wild women are too smart to sabotage productive relationships.
- **Establish strong communication skills and boundaries from the outset.** You can't blame people for things they're unaware of or uninformed of (the skillful speech mints come in handy here!).
- **Do lots of listening**, and remember that what you hear is not necessarily what your partner thinks he or she is saying.

Okay, with that bit of advice out of the way, we can now consider a few magickal processes that support this commonsense list.

First Dates

Most people are a little nervous when they're going on a first date, especially a blind date. To help offset that nervousness, take this little treat with you. Begin with a small helping of candied, chopped dates. Mingle them with some walnuts for the conscious mind, and dried cranberries for courage and protection. Put them into a food storage bag and shake them, saying:

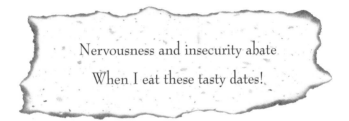

Nervousness and insecurity abate

When I eat these tasty dates!

In ancient times, dates were eaten for strength. If you're hoping for a encounter that leads to something sensual later that night, dates reputedly have a reputation for being an aphrodisiac.

Sexy Sorcery

The dating period is also the time when wild women are faced with a decision about intimacy. Every one of us has ethical codes by which we walk our talk. Sexuality should be no different. Know yourself intimately, and you'll naturally recognize when, where, and if you want to move a relationship into that arena. Additionally, you'll know how much emotion you want to give to that physical encounter. Wild women sometimes just want to have playtime (i.e., no strings attached), and that's fabulous as long as the person you're with understands the ground rules. Remember the caveat from earlier in the chapter—relationships should not be manipulated. Your intent and integrity cast a very powerful spell. That's not to say that you can't use some magick to add a dash of fun to your sexy encounters.

Desire Dust

This powder is very simple to make. You can use it on your skin, or sprinkle it around a room to create a subtle undertone of eroticism. Begin with some unscented body powder. If you want to attract a man, add a pinch of ginger powder, jasmine oil, and/or lavender oil to the base. To attract a woman, add vetivert, violet, or patchouli. You will need to mix this composition very well, dry it, and sift it again to avoid clumps. As you're creating the dust, focus on your goal and perhaps add a charm like:

Our passions inspire

kindle desire.

Repeat the charm while you're applying the powder. If you're sprinkling this in a room, vacuum it up later to remove any lingering lustful energy.

Wild women also sometimes want sensuality instead of "sexuality." Again, it's all about communication and honesty. Determine what you want, share that with the potential partner, and let nature and a little magick take its course!

Sensuality Oil

Many wild women find that a good body rub is a fantastic sensual experience that can also help put them in the "mood" after a long, busy day. To make this oil, use 2 cups of good-quality olive or almond oil. Add 1 teaspoon of orange rind (for a little luck and health), half a cinnamon stick (for an energy pick-me-up), a mint leaf (for passion and effective communication), and a few sunflower seeds (for fantasy fulfillment). Steep the components in the oil in a sunny window (for blessings and warm feelings). When it reaches an aromatic strength that you enjoy, strain it, saying:

Soothe, inspire, and heal

Soothe, inspire, and heal

Through ten helpful fingers,

This magick reveal!

Fulfill my wish,

Bring joy and zest

In this oil, be manifest!

Store the oil in an airtight container and then in a cool location until you need it. Warm it up just before you get your massage and recite your incantation to activate the spell.

Break Up, Not Apart

It would be unrealistic to assume that every dating scenario, even long-running ones, ends happily ever after. In fact, happily ever after may be highly overrated, considering its rarity. Nonetheless, the wild woman knows that each person who touches her life also changes her somehow. And if that person started as a friend, it would be a shame to lose that good rapport just because a more serious relationship didn't work out. That's why, whenever practical, the wild woman chooses to break up, not apart. When you realize that the relationship isn't working effectively on its current level, get alone with your partner as soon as possible. Wild women face their issues head-on. However, even the most confident wild woman finds confrontation difficult especially when she doesn't want to hurt someone. That's where the following charm can help.

Courage Charm

For this charm, use a bloodstone, which is associated with bravery and fortitude. Place it in the sunlight for three hours to energize it with physical, spiritual, and mental courage. Meanwhile, gather a swatch of fabric large enough to hold the stone and about ⅛ cup of loose black tea for valor and boldness. Put both items in the fabric, saying:

> Tea and bloodstone tucked within,
>
> so my magick can begin
>
> When sprinkled to wind, water, and ground
>
> Courage and strength shall abound.

Tie the bundle with a string (use a bow so it's easy to open). Sprinkle out the tea and let the wind or water carry it outward just before speaking with your friend; keep the rock in your pocket as a magickal touchstone from which to draw extra energy when you need it.

Later, when the breakup isn't so recent, ask your former partner about having a special miniritual that honors the friendship and fully releases the romantic ties you had between you. While you can enact such a ritual alone to open the pathway for rebuilding the friendship, it's far more effective if both people take part. What you do in such a ceremony is typically highly personal, but find a way to symbolize the end of the previous intimacy and the beginning of the refreshed friendship. You may want to cut a piece of rope, or bury something for the ending, and then have small tokens to exchange, for example. Afterward, go out for coffee or a movie, or something else you enjoyed doing together as friends before things got more complicated. While you're out, slowly begin to rein in your feelings. Remember what it was like when things were fun and lighthearted. Be patient with yourself. Although emotions will not disappear overnight, you can channel them into a fantastic friendship that's filled with respect.

Long-Term Relationships

Long-term relationships are like a garden. They need to be sowed, fertilized, weeded, and watered to grow beautifully. Even if you're doing all of those things, storms can come along and jostle things up. That's part of what makes a long-term relationship both difficult and rewarding.

The Garden of Love

This is a bit of old-time gardening magick that I really enjoy. To begin, you need three seeds from a flowering plant that speaks to you of love. You'll also need a red-colored planter, good potting soil, and an amethyst crystal (for nurturing love). Name the seeds after yourself, your partner, and your overall relationship (the sacred We). Every day as you tend the seeds, speak gentle, encouraging words into the soil. Talk about your wishes for your relationship, and let those wishes grow to maturity in rich soil. Meanwhile, begin sharing those wishes and hopes with your partner, and finding ways to work on them together. By the time the seeds fully blossom, you should notice an improvement in the level of emotion present in your relationship.

Word Power for Relationships

Witchy wild women are intimately aware that words have tremendous power to heal or harm depending on the intention with which they are wielded. The tape-recording activity is very helpful in changing negative habits in this regard. Another good activity is to make it a point, once a day, to say something helpful, hopeful, and uplifting to your partner. Think of it as a verbal kiss.

This activity produces several good effects. Your partner will know he or she is appreciated, and you'll be reminded daily of those things that encouraged your love in the first place—which is all too easy to lose sight of when you hit bumps in the road of your relationship.

Better still, building awareness will prove helpful to your spiritual connection together!

Tip: Pay attention to how you speak about yourself and your partner for one whole day. Tape-record yourself if possible. You'll be amazed by what you learn.

Forgiveness Ritual

When your relationship hits a bumpy spot that you both want to leave in the past, a forgiveness ritual can work wonders. Rituals, by their nature, build a bridge for us and assist with closure. To enact one, begin by meeting your partner on neutral territory and bring a breakable symbol of your anger and hurt with you. Next, each of you should share what bothered him or her the most about what happened. As you do, channel all those feelings into the symbol. It is very important to direct the negativity toward the object, and not toward each other! When each is done, jointly break those symbols and dispose of them. As you do, you can say something like this together three times:

Anger and hurt released

Hostilities ceased

Where negativity once resided

Let healing and love abide.

Promise not to bring the matter up again in the future. It's dead and buried. Turn your backs and walk away together. Do not look back. Now do something together that will help the healing process along

Unity Cup

Among the Celts and several other ancient peoples, the sharing of a single cup was one way to illustrate unity and harmony. You can do this too, and make a special magick potion with which to fill the cup! Some of the ingredients known to support loving intention include strawberries (sacred to Freya, the goddess of love and marriage), oranges (for fidelity and the health of your relationship), ginger (for a little sexy zest), and vanilla (for sensuality). You can juice these items together (3 oranges, about 1 cup of sliced strawberries, a pinch of ginger, and a hint of vanilla), straining the blend once. Bless it as you pour it into the cup, saying:

Togetherness and unity, love and beauty

Joy and peace—may they never cease

And a flirtatious wink—all within this drink!

Now drink from that singular cup and enjoy each other!

Summary

Finally, make quality time for each other; make even small moments count. In our frenzied world, it's often those small moments that make the difference between success and failure in our relationships. These moments are what I call relationship maintenance minutes. For example, when you're passing your mate in the house, touch him or her gently or give a little kiss. Or, put on your mate's favorite music and turn off the TV for a while. Over time, such efforts become more natural and help keep love full and strong.

Seven

Turnabout Is Fair Play

When among wild beasts, if they
menace you, be a wild beast.

—Herman Melville

ild women do not take it lightly when life's circumstances make them feel as lowly as an entryway rug. Nor do they simply turn the other cheek when people purposely inflict harm. We don't like the words *I can't* and hate hearing the word *no*. Now, this doesn't mean being so fervent that we overlook signals from the Universe, or ignore another's free will, but it does mean living far more proactively. It also means being willing to be a warrior woman as necessary.

Think of Joan of Arc and Lady Godiva, both of whom laid everything on the line for the things they believed in wholeheartedly. This is a part of the heart of the wild woman—a yearning to be where the action is. If that's not possible, then at the very minimum, you'll want to have some say in what transpires!

Our lives, however, don't always cooperate. That's where magick can step in and fill some gaps. It can operate forward and backward in time, and over long distances, as long as we maintain a strong will and focus. With that in mind, this chapter talks about using our craft effectively when we feel we've been wronged, when we want to turn the tables, and regain control of the driver's seat in our life's vehicle.

Cursing and Blessing

It has often been said that in order to bless, one must also know how to curse. I happen to agree with this principle; it reflects the necessity for balance in the Universe. It also illustrates that magick is a double-edged sword that can be used to create positive as well as negative energy. When creating a curse to turn the tables on a foe, a savvy wild woman must balance history against modern realities and ethics. Our ancestor's lives were much harsher and they were far less aware of scientific causes, thus superstition was more abundant. Therefore, they were more apt to retaliate against someone suspected of wrongdoing, without much thought to potential consequences. Typically, witches and wild women of old would employ curses for very specific reasons such as:

- Achieving victory over an enemy
- Recovering a stolen item from a thief
- Turning a curse against them or their property back upon its maker
- Retaliating against a stray lover

Truthfully, the idea that what you put out returns to you threefold is a far more modern concept than curses, and we must consider our ancestors' actions accordingly. It is up to every wild woman to take responsibility for her actions and decide when and if to utilize curses at all. A strong sense of self and clearly defined boundaries are critical in using this type of magick. For example, you may decide that you are able to turn the other cheek if someone hurts you but woe betide the individual who harms your family and loved ones; they will get a dose of "instant karma." However, there are some pragmatic guidelines to taking such action:

- **Calm down and think things through**. The saying "haste makes waste" comes to mind here. Anger and stress do not help the intent of your magick. In fact, they muddle the results. Take ample time to reconsider what you're doing and why.
- **Consider alternatives**. Is there anything you can do to resolve the situation? Very often, mundane solutions are actually more satisfying than magickal ones because you can quantify them more readily.
- **Be sure of the source**. You don't want to harm an innocent party in the heat of the moment. Also, be sure the harm inflicted was purposeful and not an accidental side effect of something else.
- **Visit like for like**. If you decide that some type of magickal retaliation is in order, remember that karma is all about balance. This isn't the time to embellish. If

someone harmed you financially, only focus on his or her finances in your spellcraft.

- **Add the universal clause into charms, spells, and rituals—i.e., "for the good of All" or "for the greatest good, and it harm none."** This lets the Universe step in if you're on the wrong track, or if the outcome might hurt innocents.

Please know that it is not my intention to encourage negative energy. I agree with magickal theorists who propose that similar energy will be attracted back to the practitioner—in other words, you get back what you put out (again, the principle of universal balance). However, life's circumstances sometimes press us into corners and put our backs against the wall. Those are the moments when we find our options wanting, and when considering a magickal alternative might prove very helpful. The rest of this chapter gives you some sound examples of magick that's aimed at managing some of life's more difficult moments.

Eye It Up

In olden times, the evil eye was believed to be the ability to cast a curse on someone with only a look. However, I think there are better applications for it in the wild woman's agenda. You can use a knowing glance to inspire honesty, a cool stare to quench the fires of anger, a calming look to motivate confidence, or a fervent squint to trigger culpability. The key to manifesting this ability is tied into will, focus, and a little dramatic aptitude.

The first step is to think about your goal and the best facial expressions to use to express that goal. Remember that your body is a magickal tool through which every movement can become a conduit for energy. Focus wholly on that goal until it's all that fills your mind. Turn toward the person or situation at which you want to project energy. Make sure you have a clear, direct line of sight so you don't accidentally involve the wrong person or place.

Imagine beams of light streaming from your eyes in a color appropriate to the goal (such as blue to quell anger, white for protection, yellow for improved communication). Hold your intent for several minutes and continue to visualize energy emanating from your eyes until you feel the energy connect with the person or situation you are focusing on. This feels like a telephone line where your "ring" has been received. Now let go of your end of the connection—the remaining energy you've built up will naturally follow the line you created.

Abating Anger

In Eastern martial arts, students are taught to wait and let their opponents' energy work against them, especially their anger. Similarly, we wild women know that anger throws us off balance and can actually undermine all we hope to accomplish. Therefore having a magickal coping mechanism for ire is a very good idea!

Anger is associated with fire, so elementally the way to balance fire is by using water or ice. To begin, you'll need a small flammable item that represents the person or situation who is the subject of your anger. If you can't find such an item, write its name on a piece of paper. Next, focus on your feelings and let all of them pour into the paper or item. Light it with a match and put it in a fire-proof container to burn itself out. As it does, direct your energy toward releasing any remaining negative feelings.

Now transfer the ashes into a small container (like an ice cube tray) and cover it with water. As you place the item in the freezer, you can add an incantation like:

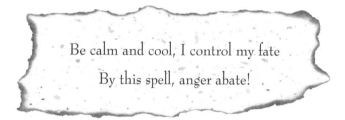

Be calm and cool, I control my fate
By this spell, anger abate!

Leave the item in the freezer until the situation that's causing your anger is completely resolved.

Slow-Down Spell

Feel as though a situation is running out of control and that things are moving too swiftly for you to find your footing? Try this spell.

First, you'll need an image of the situation or person you want to slow down. Put it on a piece of paper and draw a yellow circle around it; then a red circle around the yellow one. The circles and colors are both associated with slowing and stopping. As you draw the first circle, say:

> Slow down, slow down
> By this spell, your pace is bound.

As you draw the second circle, repeat the incantation from the first and add:

> Your pace is bound, by will constrained
> By my words, progress wanes!

Now put the paper into the soil somewhere away from your home, but in a place you go to regularly. Put a heavy rock on top to hold it in place. Once things have slowed to a comfortable pace, return and take the rock off. When you're sure the pace will remain steady, you can take out the image and burn it to stop the spell.

Healing a Broken Heart

Even the wisest person has had at least one relationship that just didn't work out. Whenever you invest your emotions, breakups hurt and leave you feeling vulnerable, angry, and unfocused. Needless to say, this won't help your quest to empower and manifest your wild woman, nor will it help your spiritual pursuits. So how do you go about healing your heart?

It is okay to let yourself grieve, provided you don't drown in it. Sometimes in our passions we forget that no person is an island and that it's completely natural to feel bad about a relationship that goes awry. Crying acts as a natural cleansing mechanism, and it releases a lot of pent-up stress. So have a good cry, and do something physical to release those feelings. This process is vitally important to recreating and rebirthing your wild woman so you can hit the social scene when you're ready.

On a spiritual level, you can create a magick balm that will help the healing process along. To make this balm, begin with any unscented cream. Add three drops of rose water (for self-love), reciting the following:

Heal my body
Heal my mind
Heal my spirit
In this cream, my magick bind!

Apply this cream daily to the area over your heart as well as to your temples and third eye (which is located in the center of your forehead). This ritual engages the body, mind, and spirit. Visualize a peaceful blue-white light filling you from head to toe and gently spreading that healing energy to every cell in your body. Use the cream as long as you have a need.

What Goes Around Comes Around

There are times in your life when you know that someone has consciously tripped you up. However, if you cannot determine the exact source of your troubles, trying magick isn't a wise choice unless you've got a sound formula. In this instance, you need to construct your spell, charm, or ritual in such a way that it's directed toward that "unknown."

Go somewhere private. Envision the situation that has caused you stress or harm. Close your eyes and breathe deeply. Try to disassociate your feelings from the matter as much as possible. What's most important here is to bring to mind as many details as you can. As you get a firm and clear image, begin to whisper:

By my will, and magick's creed
Visit the source of this evil deed
And with the law of three by three
Justice be done, the magick is freed!

Let your voice naturally grow in strength. As you do, you'll feel the energy filling you from your stomach upward. Release that power out from your hands toward the sky and let the universal spirit of justice handle it from that point onward.

Work Worries

The economic climate has been very difficult in recent years. Many people find themselves worried about job security or pay cuts. These worries put a serious kink in the wild woman's style and leave us stressed out and overextended. And while hard work can be its own good magick, there's nothing wrong with using a spell or two to protect your job or keep you working steadily with the least amount of unemployment. I add that caveat because sometimes the work we think we should be doing and where our talents would be best utilized are two different things.

In either case when you feel insecure, try making this charm and carrying it with you. You need four squares of fabric about 3" × 3": one each in white, yellow, silver, and gold. Ball up the white and yellow pieces and secure them with a string or yarn. Next, lay the silver and gold pieces on a flat surface. Place one square of cloth on top of the other one and arrange them so the points of the fabric make an eight-pointed star. This is a double-Earth sign for foundations and security. Place the ball you created from the white and yellow pieces in the center, and wrap the silver and gold pieces around it. As you secure it with string, say something like this:

White and yellow, silver and gold,

Security keep, security hold

With this charm I'll have no fears

Protect my job, protect my career!

Keep this token somewhere safe where you work.

Gossip Go Away

Among the items on a wild woman's "not if I can help it" list is gossip. This particular human behavior typically springs from jealousy, misinformation, ego, a desire to harm, or other negatives the wild woman prefers to avoid. Gossip harms; truth heals. Nonetheless, there are times when gossip gets out of control and threatens to take over a situation without any concern for what is "real" or "true." When that happens, it's time for the wild witch to get busy!

The best component for this spell is a pair of wax lips (you can often find them in old-fashioned candy stores). If you can't find them, use a picture of lips cut from a magazine. In either case, you want a black piece of yarn with which to tie the lips closed. Wrap the yarn around the lips to keep them shut symbolically. As you do this, add an incantation like this:

> Lies upon your lips be sealed
>
> From this day forward, only truth revealed
>
> Today rumors cease
>
> This spell's released!

Keep the amulet with you when you're around those you believe have been perpetuating the rumor. Burn it when the situation resolves itself.

Enemy Enmity

The concept of perfect love and trust goes only so far, especially considering that human beings are far from perfect. It's naive to think that we will love, let alone like, everyone we meet. It's also shortsighted to think that all our acquaintances will be friends. Life's circumstances often leave enmity between people no matter how much we might wish otherwise. When you find you have such a person in your life, this spell helps safeguard you from any negative energy he or she may direct toward you.

To begin, you'll need five coins (silver-toned coins are best for protection). Try to find those minted in the year of your birth for a stronger personal connection. Bless these coins one at a time using the following incantations:

Coin One

Protective Powers of the East,

Safeguard my communications

From the greatest to the least,

When called upon, your magick release!

Coin Two

Protective Powers of the Fire

Safeguard my body

Burn brightly when danger is dire

When called upon, bring clarity to the mire!

Coin Three

Protective powers of the West

Safeguard my heart

Hear my urgent request

When called upon, honor Spirit's behest!

Coin Four

Protective Powers of the Soil

Safeguard my home

And where I toil

When called upon, this spell uncoils!

Coin Five

> God and Goddess, Ancestors All
>
> Safeguard my soul
>
> Heed my earnest call
>
> When trouble threatens, be a protective wall
>
> So mote it be.

Place the first four coins somewhere in your home as close to the four cardinal directions as possible. Carry the fifth one with you as often as possible.

Truth Telling

Most people aren't really ready to hear or speak the truth. Sometimes the truth is harsh; sometimes it's just not good news. Nonetheless, wild women prefer the truth, and many of life's circumstances require that we have a clear vision of what's going on so we can act or choose wisely. When you're feeling as though you're not getting the whole truth in a situation, try this two-part spell.

The first part is to make an eyebright wash. (You can get eyebright at an herb shop or garden nursery.) This flower is associated with psychic aptitude; that is, seeing what is really there, not just what we want to see.

Simply dip the flower in some warm water and then dab the water on your eyelids and third eye, saying:

> Truth be seen, truth be told
>
> Before my eyes, the truth unfolds.

The second part of the spell begins with sunflower seeds, an agate stone, and some type of small portable container. Both sunflowers and agate improve our ability to see through the veils of life and perceive more clearly. Put the sunflower seeds and agate in the container, reciting:

> Grains of truth grow in me
>
> Charged by this agate, the magick is freed!
>
> When upon my lips this spell repeats
>
> Truth unfolds within these treats!

Eat a few of the seeds and repeat the incantation to activate honest energy in and around you.

Cooling Passion

Wild women tend to be very passionate, and sometimes those passions can overcome sound judgment. Sometimes the passions directed toward us are overwhelming, unwanted, or unhealthy. In either case, here is a handy spell to help with that!

Begin by getting a witch hazel tincture (you can find this at most drugstores). Besides being a cleanser, witch hazel tempers passion. If you're enacting this spell for yourself, then apply it to your heart chakra. If you're enacting it in an effort to encourage "cooling off" in another person, you'll want to apply it to his or her picture or to something personal. As you apply the witch hazel, repeat the following incantation four times. The first three times are directed toward body, mind, and spirit. The fourth repetition is to ground the energy in the earth.

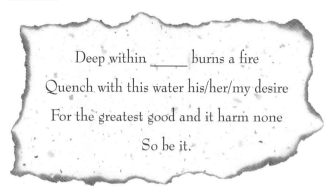

Deep within _____ burns a fire
Quench with this water his/her/my desire
For the greatest good and it harm none
So be it.

Fill in the blank with the name of the person toward whom the spell is directed.

Recharging

I know there are days when I feel as limp and lifeless as a wet noodle. Wild women are typically very busy, often wearing many hats and giving a whole new meaning to multitasking. Consequently, it's easy for us to run our batteries down. Needless to say, that simply won't do. Not only does it leave you susceptible to illness, but it zaps your magick spark. So get proactive and utilize good humor and good spellcraft to help yourself along.

A dear friend of mine gave me some great advice when I was feeling really burned out. His advice on recharging (with some minor adaptations) goes like this:

1. Put on a totally irreverent T-shirt—something you know will make people stop before they bug you.

2. Grab your favorite comfort foods and a beverage. Take them in front of a TV; move everything but your goodies and a remote to an arm's length away.

3. Cast a circle using an invocation like:

To the East: I give no shit and expect none in return.

To the South: I am hungry, light the hearth fires and feed me junk food!

To the West: Life is good; let only good vibes flow or else! Bring me drink!

(It helps to look at anyone who lives in your space with you with a truly wicked stare at this point.)

To the North: This is my seat from which to channel surf. I have the buttons of power. Do not mess with me.

To Spirit: All-great Couch Potato in the sky, I know I have erred in my ways. It is time to cease laboring for eight days a week, and enjoy a sitcom. For the next few hours the words *guilt, diet, work,* and *stress* shall not be upon my tongue. And let all assembled agree by saying HELL YEAH!

Now, just sit in the chair, twitch occasionally, and speak in tongues whenever anyone dares come close. How many times you need to repeat this ritual depends on the degree to which you have been completely sucked dry. The more you do this ritual, the faster the responses for your spirit will be.

Summary

Don't forget that serious magick should be balanced with a fair amount of humor. Serious magick is for serious situations when everything else has failed you, while amusement is a great coping mechanism for life's hassles. Laugh and the world laughs with you, as the saying goes. The wild woman tries to laugh daily because she knows it is good soul food—as well as the best way to turn the tables on those who tried to ruin her good spirits in the first place!

Eight

The Archetypal Wild Woman

Time has been transformed, and we have changed; it has advanced and set us in motion; it has unveiled its face, inspiring us with bewilderment and exhilaration.

—Kahlil Gibran

*A*nytime you set out on a new or different path, the journey is often met and undertaken with excitement and uncertainty. You are hopeful, but you know little about the road ahead. Will it be smooth? Will there be detours and potholes? Will it truly lead you to where your spirit yearns to go?

As with so many things in life, until you attempt the adventure, you will never know for certain what it will bring. There are, however, models to whom you can look in taking that first, big step. Throughout world mythology, history, and lore, all manner of wild women have provided enduring inspiration. Their "her-stories" reveal how a person who chooses to think and live differently can have a huge impact—not just in her own life, but in the world.

This preface will take you on a brief global exploration of wild, bawdy, and even wanton women. Specifically we'll learn about goddesses who lived so much outside their societal boxes that their stories impact us thousands of years later. As you read about them, please realize you don't have to take your life to the same extremes to discover and reactivate the wild woman inside yourself. Rather the idea here is to find some good archetypes and characteristics on which to focus in order to develop your unique personalized reflection of this liberating energy.

Sexual, Orgiastic, and Pleasure Goddesses

One interesting trait of nearly every wild woman I've ever known, or about whom I've read, is that she knows that her body is sacred. Additionally, she has no guilt associated with pleasure and no shame in enjoying her physical expression to the fullest. If anything, wild women celebrate the wonders of the body and explore them to discover how best to tease and please, not just others but themselves too!

Mind you this exploration and celebration has some limits. No, not those set by society, family, or some outmoded view of sexual rights and roles, but rather those created by common sense and each woman's personal code. Beginning with common sense, it was very likely a wild woman who first came up with the idea of safe sex. After all, it was the cunning woman of most villages who knew how to prepare cleansing herbs and abortive potions. However wild woman know that the concept of safe sex extends to more than just protecting their physical health; it's also about safeguarding emotions, as well as a very pragmatic way of honoring your temple—your body! A truly aware wild woman knows that an energy exchange occurs during a physical relationship. She realizes she will be changed, if only a bit, from the encounter. Once the intention is set and expectations are clarified, the wild woman can relax and release herself to the moment and the pleasures it offers. So, who are some of the archetypes to consider for this part of our journey? Let's take a look:

Achtland (Celtic): A mortal queen who found human men inadequate to her tastes. To satisfy her, she married a giant whose hair she loved to comb. Achtland may have been a bit of a proverbial-size queen, but she knew what she wanted and needed, and then found a way to fulfill both!

Agave (Greece): A daughter of Harmonia, who with her sister established the Bacchantes—a women's only group whose rites included dancing, drinking, music, and hunting. The purpose here was to release the wildness within to become ecstatically part of life's divinity. If any man invaded their rituals, he was beheaded. Talk about marking your territory!

Aisha Quandisha (Morocco): A beautiful Spirit with goat legs who enjoyed seducing young men, even though she already had a consort. This was a goddess who reached for diversity and new experiences with gusto.

Anat (Ugaritic): The mistress of all gods who never lost her hymen throughout her wanton affairs. She remained independent and pure, no matter how many people she took to bed. The lesson here is clear—your body is your sacred space. No one *owns* your body— you choose whom you share it with, whom you let in, and whom you keep firmly out.

Antianara (Amazon): A queen who kept crippled male slaves, feeling they were the best to provide her with acts of love. Antianara reminds us that there is much more to our partners than the exterior.

Arianrhod (Celtic): A sorceress-goddess who liked to mate with mermen. She is sometimes depicted as pretending to be a virgin. Her story is somewhat tragic in that she eventually created more energy than she could handle responsibly and her island broke to pieces, killing all her servants. Arianrhod reminds us that we need to know our limits and be proactive in understanding the potential consequences of our actions.

Asherah (Canaan): A lady of the sea who was celebrated with orgiastic rites. She was always regarded as being kind and present in any public pleasures. Beyond this, she suckled the gods, provided oracles to humans, and embodied life's force. Asherah's message is uplifting in that it honors the life-giving power of sex but also recognizes it as a unique pleasure to be enjoyed fully.

Astarte (Near East): A fiercely independent and untamed goddess of sexuality who is often associated with Venus. She's depicted riding naked on a lioness. Her colors are red and white, her trees are acacia and cypress, and a stallion was her sacred animal. It's appropriate to offer her the first fruits of the harvest when calling on her to inspire personal liberation.

Dakini (Hindu): Dakini were the attendants of Kali, consort to the Hindu god, Shiva. These female spirits carry a very powerful energy that humans can connect with in spiritual practices, such as Kundalini work

Eos (Greece): The goddess of dawn, Eos enjoyed taking many lovers, one of whom was Orion the mighty hunter and son of Poseidon, god of the sea. Even with such experiences, Eos fell in love with a mortal whom she asked the gods to make immortal, which they did although they did not give him eternal youth. When her mate became old, she turned him into a cricket so that he could sing to her each day as she left to bring light to the world. So it would seem that wild women, while having strong independent streaks, also have a sense of devotion and loyalty toward those they keep close to their hearts.

Ezili-Freda-Dahomey (Haiti): The voodoo goddess of sensuality who gives liberally to those who likewise offer liberally. She is a good teacher for learning how to give and receive (physically, mentally, and spiritually) with equal graciousness.

Hit (Micronesia): A sky goddess who used her wanton dances to keep a god's wife (Sky Woman) from interfering in her daughter's love affair. Apparently Hit's dances were so wild that the Sky Woman would faint at the sight of them. No one knows for sure if it was shock, or if Sky Woman found herself attracted to Hit, but in either case Hit knew how to use her body effectively!

Kunti (India): The Earth goddess who could accept all manner of men into herself without ever being transformed by their energy. Kunti is another example of the wild woman who retains her sense of self, her independence, and sees no need to lose herself in a union.

Maeve (Ireland): A beloved goddess who often appears inebriated. Nonetheless, she ran swifter than horses and was offered the bed of kings; no man who looked upon her could refuse her anything. Did all that beauty come with a price? A lot of pressure and expectation surrounds physical beauty, perhaps that's why Maeve took to drinking so much wine!

Pele (Hawaii): The fires of this goddess were almost her undoing. She fell in love with a mortal with whom she made love for three years. Upon returning to her mountain home, Pele sent her sister Hiiaka to safely fetch her mate. While her sister was away, Pele's jealousy began to imagine the worst. In her fury she destroyed Hiiaka's favorite poet and gardens, even though Hiiaka had been wholly faithful to her sister. Hiiaka responded by making love to the mortal, who had also fallen in love with Hiiaka on the journey. Finally seeing how her passions had destroyed so much, Pele relented and gave Hiiaka her lover. Pele's message? Understand and control your jealousy and passions; do not let them control you!

Qadesh (Egypt): An Egyptian goddess who appears on a lion's back, sometimes wearing a headpiece that implies pleasure. In her worship, sex was regarded with all due reverence as a kind of sacrament that produced

Divine energy. This is an excellent goddess to draw inspiration from when thinking about symbolic or literal sexual rites.

Uzume (Japan): A goddess who used a humorous striptease to bring the sun goddess Amaterasu out of hiding so life could return to the world. The gods so enjoyed her performance that they laughed and clapped with pleasure. Uzume's story shows wild women that there is always a place for play and joy in the bedroom.

Xochiquetzal (Aztec): Similar to Fauna in many ways, Xochiquetzal is filled with sexual and fertile energy. This was a beloved goddess who seemed to adore all living things especially those that blossomed. It was she and one man who, after the flood, took on the task of re-establishing all of humankind to the world. In Xochiquetzal we get a combination mother-mate image that's very positive and filled with abundance.

Nature-Dwelling Spirits and Teachers

When we use the term *wild,* we must also consider it in terms of nature. The wild within is tied to our animal self, to our tribal past, and to Earth and all its creatures. Getting to know that rawness, tapping that unbridled yet coherent order of things, discovering that sheer sense of *being* is an inherent effect of activating and enabling your wild woman.

To fill out this corner of the portrait for wild women, I'm turning to Buschfrauen. In Europe, these mythic wild women lived in hollow trees. They had three rules. First, they didn't bake caraway into bread, because spirits could not eat it. In this, they honored all aspects of the world, both the seen and unseen. Second, they didn't take bark from the trees, because it left the tree exposed to disease. This practice honored nature and its gifts. Third, they would not tell a person their dreams, which was a way of honoring self. When the Buschfrauen were pleased with humans, they taught them secrets of the herbal and agrarian arts, especially those for crop growth and healing. In other words, they gave to worthy individuals, specifically those who held similar ethics.

The Polish version of the Buschfrauen are called Dziwozony. Rather than living in trees, these nature spirits sought shelter underground. This housing is very telling in that it reveals the Dziwozony preferred to be as close to Earth's "womb" as possible when seeking to understand nature's language and secrets. And like their Buschfrauen counterparts, the Dziwozony had herbal curative knowledge. So we see that the wild woman's quest to reacquaint herself with Earth's gifts and lessons comes with viable rewards, an innate knowledge of how to use nature's pharmacy and supermarket!

Humorous and Playful Deities

Let it never be said that a wild woman is boring, apathetic, monotonous, or downright dull. Laughter is soul food for her, and play is a fabulous way to release the stresses of the nine-to-five world. Nonetheless, it sometimes seems that many spiritual people have lost their ability to laugh at life and to laugh at themselves. They get so serious and dogmatic that they lose their joy. Magick is the ability to revel.

One lesson from the wild woman's book of wisdom is that fun is functional. We tend to forget that as children playtime produced a great many of life's lessons, such as how to dress up for make-believe, how to climb a tree without falling, or how to ride a bike without scraping knees. Playtime gave us insights into our own abilities and how to manage everyday challenges. Magical living is like that, too. We can have fun and still be learning and growing in the process. In fact, I'd say it's nearly sinful for a wild woman *not* to have fun regularly. Here are five goddesses whose jobs were, in part, to remind us of just that:

Bast (Egypt): A fertile, friendly, and frolicsome cat goddess, she found pleasure in dance, song, and revelry. When her followers enjoyed themselves and gave of their talents at celebrations, Bast blessed them with health. See, playing *is* good for your body!

Baubo (Greece): Her name literally translated means "belly." This goddess of laughter was also very suggestive in her jokes. Baubo's humor and her sister Iambe's words brought the goddess Demeter out of a long streak of sadness when her daughter was missing. This laughter gave hope to the darkened world.

Iambe (Greece): The goddess of bawdy speech, Iambe helped Baubo give Demeter joy in her time of sorrow and was basically a good companion during her time of need. Iambe shows us that the wild woman's clever tongue can be a great gift to those around her.

Sheila na Gig (Ireland): An ever-smiling old woman, Sheila na Gig is not simply the goddess of humor, but also of sadness, of life and death, and of sex and celibacy. Her frequent depiction as a woman holding open her vagina for the world to see is symbolic of life's passages, while her wrinkles also remind us of our mortality. Sheila na Gig's message is a simple one: There is a time for all things.

Siduri (Assyria-Babylonia): An aspect of Ishtar, the mother goddess, the charge of this goddess is very simple: to dance and play and make each day joyful. I couldn't have said it better myself!

Wild Warriors

Wild women move through all walks of life and come from many backgrounds. However, one thing they have in common is a low tolerance level for bullshit. Life is too short to divert copious amounts of time or energy to those things that aren't positive and life affirming. Life is also too short to allow people to abuse kindness, twist charity, manipulate weakness, or scandalize shortcomings. Thus, many times the wild woman finds herself in the role of warrior and protector, for herself and for others who aren't quite as actualized or aware (at least not yet). So what is it that draws out this warrior spirit? Typically this aspect of the wild woman comes out during disruptions, chaos, emergencies—in other words, she's activated by *need*. In a moment of need, when her authority and position is unquestioned, the wild warrior does her utmost to defend truth, honor, freedom, and other similar values that she holds dear. Because of this and the rather unexpected nature of life, the warrior aspect of the wild woman must always be prepared to come to the fore, but she must balance that readiness against knowing which battles are truly hers to fight. She must also be attentive, awake, and aware of herself and her surroundings. Or to put it more precisely, she must control those surroundings and how she responds to each moment.

Here are just a few women warriors to whom we can look for inspiration:

Aella (Greece): This feisty Amazon fended off the Greek invaders in an effort to protect her queen. Her name means "whirlwind." Talk about the ultimate in the proverbial "winds of change"!

Aigiarm (Mongolia): A princess who could win in battle against any man who challenged her. Typically she would bet she could overcome suitors in wrestling matches, offering her virginity as wager. The men had to promise their horses if they lost. Lore tells us that she won 10,000 horses! Come to her when you feel challenged by a masculine force that seems overwhelming.

Atalanta (Arcadia): Atalanta grew up in the forest and was raised by a she-bear. This gave her great strength and an instinctive nature, which she used to battle centaurs. People saw her as a great heroine, and a great beauty, yet she refused to marry any man who was not her equal or better, which the wild woman can take as great advice for any relationship!

Cyrene (Greece): A princess who was not content to live life on the sidelines, Cyrene is described as being very adept with a sword and javelin. She wrestled lions as a hobby. Although lion wrestling may not have much relevance in the modern world, the wild woman typically finds some sort of physical outlet through which she can express her strengths and perspectives.

Galiana (Etruscan): A great heroine who used pure shock value to defend her home city from the Romans. She bravely came to the battlements totally naked. This apparently had a spell-like effect and the Romans retreated. Ladies, never be afraid of the power of your sexuality, but use it wisely.

Hyrrokin (Scandinavia): Upon the death of his son, Balder, the god of light could think of nothing other than his grief. Thus, the death-ship that traveled to the underworld ceased to sail. To remedy this situation, the gods brought this giant woman who used raw muscle to relaunch Balder's ship and send it on its way. Call on her to get things moving in your life!

Jingo (Japan): A great leader who myths claim stayed pregnant for three years in order to finish her campaign on Korea. Under her command, all of the Korean territory was undone, and promised her fealty. Jingo's lesson is determination, and how it can (and will) eventually bring respect.

Macha (Ireland): A fierce and brave goddess who was so fast she beat horses in a foot race. She even did so (at her husband's behest) when pregnant with twins. Sadly this effort killed her. Before she died, however, she cursed her husband and all men of Ulster for their boasting and betting. Here is an example of a woman whose gifts were abused. Heed her lesson and do not let people take you for granted.

Nessa (Ireland): A warrior figure, Nessa kept fully involved in all matters of government. When one of the Ulster men raped her, she remained his concubine until she bore a great hero, who was not his son but a child of magick. The child eventually became king and her protector. Here, the wild warrior is shown as a good strategist who knows her own mind and definitely has her own agenda!

Oya (Brazil): A Santerian warrior goddess who presides over both fire and matters of justice. Oya's lesson is that spiritual justice and human justice do not always mix. The wise warrior works within the laws of the world but sees the bigger picture.

Pherenice (Greece): An interesting historical figure, Pherenice decided to teach her son wrestling, even to the point of disguising herself at the Olympics. He won, and she was eventually honored for her coaching skill. Wild warriors dare to dream, and then they make those dreams come true!

Scathach (Scotland): A great warrior to whom others turned to learn battle arts including magickal leaps and shouts that would insure success. This is an excellent goddess to whom to turn should you decide to study martial arts.

Telesilla (Greece): This woman was a muse and poet who managed to fight her way out of a Spartan siege at Argos, leading a large group of other warrior women. Not bad for a poet! In this case we see that the wild warrior has more than just swords at her disposal—her words, her actions, and her thoughts all have power.

Thorgerd (Iceland): A highly protective goddess who would awaken to defend her people from any threat. Each of her fingers bore an arrow that would kill without fail. She also presided over nature, being called upon for success in both hunting and fishing expeditions. Thorgerd teaches us that a warrior's job is not simply one of defense but also one of sustenance. What do you need to sustain your sacredness?

Trung Trac (China): A historical figure captured as a goddess by mythology, Trung Trac bravely led her people against a despot governor. Being successful, she became their queen. Trung Trac is a goddess who shows us the kinds of fights that are worthy of our effort and attention.

Yatiaz (Mongolia): A heroine who went to the heavens to implore the chief god's daughters to restore her brother to life. To achieve her goal, she had to compete in numerous physical trials, all of which she won. Here we see that the warrior can find great strength in love.

Goddesses Worshiped and Consulted by Women

Last but certainly not least in our exploration, we come to goddesses who were favored predominantly by women. If such goddesses captured the attention of our ancestors, whose lives were much harsher than ours, they must be worthy of our attention today! Although there were certainly many more than can be listed here, these five give you a place to begin:

Bona Dea (Rome): A pleasant goddess also known as Fauna, Bona Dea was frequently worshiped by women. Bona Dea's attributes include prosperity and prophetic ability, which is in keeping with the intuitive feminine archetype.

Ishtar (Near East): A multifaceted goddess considered the embodiment of womanhood and benevolence, Ishtar battled with anyone who tried to take away her independence and was sought as both an advisor and judge. Ishtar is an excellent helpmate when you need to make sound choices, or when you need to deal with legal matters.

Mylitta (Phoenicia): The priests of this goddess's tradition welcomed those who wished to perform sacred acts of love. Women would often come to her shrine and wait for a pleasing mate. Mylitta's message: There are always choices to make, so choose what makes you happy and retains your Sacred Self.

Paphos (Greece): A name for Aphrodite and any of her followers who have devoted their bodies to the goddess's service. Some women who choose to remain independent of a mate will find Paphos a great advocate.

Summary

Books examining heroines and goddesses of the world have thousands upon thousands of entries. Many of these deities exemplify the wild woman we're working toward becoming. Consequently, you may want to read more and learn more about those who have come before you on this path. Each time you find one of these brave, bold women, consider what lessons and examples she embodies.

If you choose to call on some of these deities to aid in your path and magick, I advise getting to know that goddess more intimately. Just as you would not go up to a stranger's door, walk in, and grab a beer, knocking on a goddess's door and making requests is a bit impudent without a deeper understanding of her, the culture from which she comes, her attributes, and what things she holds sacred. Treat her with respect and interest, as you would other mortal wild women. As you do, and as your relationship with your personal goddess develops, you will naturally continue to discover more about the wild within, and how to use that energy for the greatest good...for the good of all . . . and for the good of one: you.

Nine

Celebrate the Wild Woman

Grant me some wild expressions,
Heavens, or I shall burst.
—George Farquhar

        omewhere in the world right now a festival,
holiday, or celebration is taking place that uplifts the
spirit of the wild woman. One of the most familiar
examples that comes to mind is Leap Year Day. In times
gone by, this was a day when women could toss off
societal restraints, ask men to dance, and do other bold
and daring things they would not be considered seemly
otherwise. For modern wild women, everyday is Leap
Year Day! Be that as it may, this chapter reviews other
similar holidays from around the world and associated
magickal energies they bear.

    By celebrating any one of these, you can honor the
feminine spirit, the Goddess, and begin to fully actualize
your inner wild woman. Before doing so, however, it's a
good idea to do a little research. If you find a holiday
on this list that seems to appeal to your spirit, go online
or check out your local library. That way you can get a

better idea of how the event unfolded in its native culture as well as the various traditions associated with it. Determine what traditional activities you'd like to integrate into your personal celebration of the day and what magickal processes will blend effectively with those activities. Consider what type of sensual cues you can add to improve the overall experience. For example, if you choose an oceanic celebration, you might decorate with seashells or other items that remind you of the tropics. Similarly, if you're celebrating Kwan Yin's birthday, it's helpful to find out about her traditional offerings.

In this manner, the wild woman blends the best of history and custom with modern realities and personal needs. This adaptation process shouldn't be approached recklessly; transformations are profound and meaningful. Your learning and exploration process should express gratitude toward the people and culture that originated the event. Here are a few of the celebrations and festivals that uplift and celebrate women in some manner.

Basket Dance

Associated energies: Gratitude, abundance, fertility

Celebrated by Hopi women, basket dances take place in October and November to honor the harvest and give thanks for Earth's fertility. The women dance, sing, and toss baskets (baskets being symbolic of the woman's womb) to Hopi men.

Bona Dea Festival

Associated energies: Goddess worship, sisterhood, prophecy, foresight

This festival comes to us from ancient Rome where it was celebrated on May Day. Bona Dea, whose name literally means "good day," was a matronly and prophetic goddess. Her festival was solely for women.

Carmentalia

Associated energies: Birth or beginnings, divination, fertility

Carmentalia is a Roman goddess for whom women seemed to be the primary worshipers. This makes sense considering she presided over birthing, and more specifically the art of midwifery. Her festival was held on January 11 and 15, and included offerings of grain and fortunetelling efforts.

Cerealia

Associated energies: Providence, gardening magick, self-control

Another Roman festival Cerealia was observed only by matrons who, prior to the event, abstained from wine and any carnal pleasures. Overall Cerealia was an event intended to inspire fertile fields, and it took place on April 19.

Green Corn Ceremony

Associated energies: Honoring women, gratitude, elemental magick, purification

The Green Corn Ceremony is a Greek harvest festival that takes place in late summer. It is a time for thankfulness, honoring the elements, and cleansing. Drums and rattles played by women accompany many of the rites.

Goddess of Mercy's Birthday

Associated energies: Women and children's safety, healing, kindness, compassion

Kwan Yin is among the most beloved goddesses of the East, being the Bodhisattva (Buddha-to-be) of compassion and mercy. Worshiped by the Japanese, Chinese, and Koreans, Kwan Yin hears the cries of the world, protects women and children, and can see suffering wherever it may be. Women often take Kwan Yin as a patroness, offering her fresh fruit, flowers, and cakes on her birthday, which is typically celebrated on the 19 day of the third lunar month (between March and April).

Haola

Associated energies: Fertility, friendship, revelry, sexuality

Taking place in ancient Greece in late December, women came together in a whirlwind of revelry. Lewd jokes and games, pastries fashioned to look like sexual parts, and a great deal of feasting and drinking took place in the belief that the women's friendly warmth and passions would also warm up Earth and make it fertile again.

The Festival of Juno

Associated energies: Relationships, home, love, commitment

The Festival of Juno, who was the Roman goddess of women and marriage, was celebrated on July 7. Juno oversaw every aspect of the feminine life from birth to running the household. Her sacred bird was the goose, and one of her fruits was the fig. It's no surprise that the month of June, named after her, is still the most popular month for weddings!

Kartika Snan

Associated energies: Purification, worship, house blessing

The time between October and November is a traditional time for acts of piety. Hindu women get up early to cleanse themselves in sacred streams. They then visit the temple and hang lamps that remain lit throughout the entire month, inspiring blessings. The light of the lamp is symbolic of the person's prayers shining outward and upward. It's also customary to offer tulsi leaves to Vishnu, which pleases him more than cows!

Karwachoth

Associated energies: Prosperity, longevity, blessing

Another Hindu festival that takes place during Kartika, Karwachoth is a time to honor Parvati, the goddess of prosperity and longevity. Mothers bless their married daughters on this day, but no virgins or widows may participate in the observances because it is believed to taint the fertile aspects. Fasting until the moon rises is customary.

Ladies Day at Big Iron Farm Show

Associated energies: Earth magick, creativity, transformation

This event takes place annually in September to honor and commemorate the contributions of women to rural living. It includes shows of heirloom arts, and various discussions on the changing role of women on the family farm.

Matralia

Associated energies: Children, kinship, family, new beginnings

This Roman festival took place on June 11 honoring Mater Matuta, a goddess of dawn and childbirth. Only matrons and freeborn women could participate in this event, which took place at the temple. Typically it was a time to pray for one's nieces and nephews and give offerings of flowers to an image of the goddess. An alternative date for this celebration is March 1, which was one of Juno's festival dates when married women presided over the event.

Ropotine

Associated energies: Role reversal, peace, protection

This Romanian festival takes place on the third Tuesday after Easter (which falls between April 7 and May 18). An event celebrated only by women, married women use this day to switch roles with their mates. Men become hand servants for one small chore—that of baking a special bread called tzesturi, which is given to children and needy people. It's said this bread staves off any threats of war.

Rukmani Ashtami

Associated energies: Relationships, happiness, wealth

A Hindu observance celebrated by women, this holiday takes place on the eighth day of the waning month of Pausa (December or January) to honor Rukmani's (the wife and queen of Krishna) birthday. It's customary to prepare offerings or gifts for charity on this day, as well as to abstain from eating. Those who observe the fast are then blessed with conjugal bliss and prosperity.

Saint Dominique's Day

Associated energies: Midwifery, fertility, sisterhood

In Macedonia, January 22 is this saint's feast day, but more important it's a time to honor and celebrate the ancient art of midwifery. Only women of childbearing age participate by sharing food, wine, and useful gifts with their midwife. Other activities include kissing a phallic symbol for fertility and a giant feast where women enjoy each other's fellowship with song and humor.

Savitri Vrata

Associated energies: Love, devotion, longevity

This Hindu festival takes place in May or June and is observed by married women as a means of blessing their husbands. It's based on the legend of Savitri who loved her husband so much that she refused to leave him even in death and eventually persuaded the Lord of Death to return him to her. Women spend the day fasting, praying, and anointing their mate with sandalwood oil in order to persuade the gods to grant him long life. Widows pray to be released from the misery of that loss in their future lives. Note: these particular customs could be redirected toward a female partner.

Susan B. Anthony Day

Associated energies: Tenacity, commitment to a cause, individual rights

Celebrations for this amazing woman take place on her birthday, which is February 15 or on August 26, the date the Nineteenth Amendment was ratified. Susan devoted her life to the causes of temperance, abolition of slavery, and women's suffrage.

Teej

Associated energies: Womanhood, purification, gratitude

Sometime between July and August, this Hindu festival celebrates women, and specifically the goddess Parvati (the consort to Shiva and patroness of women). Activities include decorating one's hands and feet with henna in meaningful symbols, singing songs to Parvati, cleansing in a sacred river, and giving gifts to the special women in one's life.

Thesmophoria

Associated energies: Safeguarding relationships, fertility, chastity, the harvest

This Greek festival for Demeter, goddess of fertility and protector of marriages, occurred in the fall between September and October. Women were the chief participants in this event, which lasted three days as part of harvest celebrations. Women often helped bless and fertilize fields on this day, having either fasted or abstained from sex to ensure a good harvest.

Woman's Day

Associated energies: Feminine spirit, justice, work

Internationally celebrated on March 8, this holiday commemorates working women and is among the most widely observed of more modern holidays. The date has its origins in the mid-1800s in New York when women in the garment industry protested the deplorable working conditions. Typically people around the world have special exhibitions of the contributions women have made in various fields.

Summary

I have always felt that anytime is the right time for magick. There doesn't need to be a special occasion or time frame. Similarly, wild women know that there's no specific date or time when we should celebrate and honor ourselves and the spirit of all women. In fact, our daily lives should become that act of honor, respect, and gratitude—then everything else is icing on the cake (make mine chocolate, please!). It's my sincere hope that this book has helped you tap into and enjoy that inner spirit, so that you're having a slice of that cake and eating it too! May today and every day be filled with sweetness, joy, and wild wonders! Blessed be.

Appendix: Resources

Organizations

National Council of Women's Organizations—Represents more than 200 groups representing more than 10 million women in the United States): *www.womensorganizations.org*

The Feminist Majority—This group is involved with everything from medical research and politics to reproductive rights and the arts: *www.feminist.org*

National Organization for Women—Voters' guides, the ABCs of Women's Issues, and overall proactive "watch" group for women's rights: *www.now.org*

The Guerrilla Girls—A truly wild group of women who work to expose sexism and racism wherever it may be: *www.guerrillagirls.com*

General Federation of Women's Clubs—A large and well-established group that works to support the arts, preserve natural resources, promote education, encourage healthy lifestyles, stress civic involvement, and work toward world peace and understanding: *www.gfwc.org*

International Center for Research on Women—Whose goal is to improve women's lives especially those in poverty, as well as an overall focus on human rights and social well-being: *www.icrw.org*

Women's International Center—This group honors achievement in women, offers scholarships, and supports environmental causes: *www.wic.org*

National Women's Martial Arts Federation—This group's goal is to share skills and resources while promoting excellence in the martial arts among girls and women: *www.nwmaf.org*

Woman's Organizations—A Web site dedicated to listings of various groups around the world including academic, special interest, and professional organizations: *www.library.wisc.edu/libraries/WomensStudies/orgs.htm*

Ms Foundation for Women—An equal rights activist group: *www.ms.foundation.org*

Woman's Information Network—Professional development opportunities: *www.winonline.org*

American Businesswoman's Organization—Education, networking support, and professional development: *www.abwa.org*

Online Groups

Wild Wolf Women—Focused on the book *Women Who Run with the Wolves,* exploring our "wild" side: *www.wildwolfwomen.com*

Online Women's Business Center—Interactive training site: *www.onlinewbc.gov*

Women Online Worldwide—Chats, message boards, and much more: *www.wowwomen.com*

Planet Out—Gay, lesbian, and bi chats; message boards; and education: *www.planetout.com*

Oxygen.com—Ongoing chats on a wide variety of subjects: *www.oxygen.com*

Happenings

Wiminfest—Celebration of women's arts, music, performance, and culture, held every year in Albuquerque, New Mexico: *www.wiminfest.org*

The Michigan Womyn's Music Festival—An all-womyn's cultural event held each August. Pages list the performances, workshops, events, and activities of the six-day Music Festival: *www.michfest.com*

New Hampshire Women's Music Festival—Founded in 1993, this festival is sponsored by the New Hampshire Feminist Collective: *www.nhwomensmusicfest.org*

National Women's Music Festival—A four-day musical and cultural extravaganza that tries to incorporate just about every facet of women's lives. The festival is held indoors on the campus of Ball State University in Muncie, Indiana: *http://wiaonline.org/nwmf/*

Women's festivals of music and the arts: *http://creativefolk.com/festivals.html*

LezbeOut—More listings for your consideration: *www.lezbeout.com/WomensFestivals.htm*

Twin Oaks—A Virginia gathering of women to celebrate the arts: *www.twinoaks.org/community/women/*

Women's sports events (complete listing): *www.womensportsevents.com*

Aurora 2004 Women's Event Listing—For business-women: *www.auroravoice.com/events.asp*

The Woman's Calendar—A large event listing with everything from business expos to sexual assault education: *www.womenscalendar.org*